BITE THE ASS OFF A BEAR

CONTENTS

———

FOREWORD

BY CLIFF VINER

———

Our firm, III Capital Management, is a unique place. In July 2017, we'll celebrate our 35th anniversary. Since our founding in 1982, we've witnessed a tremendous evolution in the fixed income arbitrage and derivatives business. While III is certainly a meritocracy, our partners and employees have created a legacy and culture of true collaborative effort. Our partners are paid from the same collective earnings pool, and our employees know that the better the organization performs as a whole, the more we're able to increase our compensation across the board. Everyone is incentivized to pull in the same direction.

The collaborative effort is conducted in an atmosphere of respect, friendship, and, above all, character, character,

character. And that's where Garth comes in. Garth has been with III for almost twenty years now, and he exemplifies the best of what III stands for. He began as an assistant trader but quickly proved his trading acumen, analytic abilities, and management and business development skills.

Early on, Garth dealt in US government and agency securities and US agency mortgages, hedging these various assets with Treasury futures contracts, interest rate swaps, and swaptions. He then expanded that scope to the Danish mortgage market, creating hedging techniques that did not exist prior to his entrance into that market.

Subsequent to those trading activities, Garth became a partner at III and exhibited his substantial business development capabilities by guiding III into the credit and credit derivatives business. He hired outstanding individuals of diverse credit talents, helped launch our two long/short credit vehicles, and was instrumental in creating our Credit Bias fund in 2007, which benefited greatly from its short credit exposure during the 2008 financial crisis.

Through both good times and difficult times, Garth has always shown the important personal and professional traits necessary for success. He was constantly pushing the company's collective scope of knowledge, allowing us to enter new markets, develop new expertise, and push the boundaries of fixed income and credit arbitrages.

His even-handed style and composure have been crucial to helping us maintain our particular culture. Even during 2008, a trying time for the fixed income derivatives business, we could count on Garth to deliver measured and well-thought-out assessments at our 7:00 a.m. partner strategy sessions.

Yes, Garth has seen and experienced it all in his years in the industry. His stories and personal reflections will certainly amuse and educate the reader. Ultimately, his instructions, advice, and admonitions ring true, because they come from the strength of his character. They are based on the most elevated meanings of personal success, achievement, and fulfillment. Sure, there are many paths to success. But ultimate satisfaction comes from reaching those goals and being proud of the road that got you there.

Garth has every reason to be proud of the road and direction of his career. You'll gain from his business teachings and the spirit and point of view that permeate the entire book. I wish the reader of this book much success, and I am grateful to have Garth Friesen as a partner on my own business journey.

—CLIFF VINER, FOUNDER AND CIO, III CAPITAL MANAGEMENT

INTRODUCTION

"Wall Street." People hear the words and their minds immediately race to familiar scenes from popular culture, like Gordon Gekko declaring, "Greed is good," or the raucous parties in *The Wolf of Wall Street*. Maybe they bring to mind some of the damning articles or books written about the industry in recent years, like Sam Polk's *New York Times* editorial depicting Wall Street as a den of avarice and addiction, or Michael Lewis's *The Big Short*, and his semi-autobiographical *Liar's Poker*, which portrays Wall Street as a form of legalized gambling. The media, eager to find villains for the financial crisis of 2008 have reinforced these stereotypes by sensationalizing every instance of financial malfeasance.

Ask anyone to describe a typical Wall Street trader, and they'll throw out words like *arrogance* and *excess*. They'll grumble about unwarranted bonuses going to people who got jobs because of nothing more than an Ivy League education, a well-connected father, and the old boys' club. The assumption is that once these young traders land a position, they have made it. On top of the world, they sit back and bank millions of dollars for the rest of their careers while doing little work.

With a twenty-plus year career in finance, which saw me rise from a loan processor at a small foreign bank to the Co-CIO of a $4 billion hedge fund and a member of the New York Federal Reserve's Investor Advisory Committee on Financial Markets, I can confirm that the reality is far different from the reputation.

Maybe twenty years ago trading floors were packed with traders—ties loosened, collars open, shirt sleeves rolled up—shouting out orders, cursing, slamming down phones, and verbally abusing new hires. Anyone walking onto a typical trading floor nowadays, however, would be surprised at how the atmosphere matches that of a university library. Trading is a cerebral process, and the sound of crunching keyboards is the only noise breaking the silence on the floor. If not for the four or five computer monitors on each desk, there'd be no way of knowing it was an investment firm.

Trading may be a high-stakes, high-stress world, but at the end of the day, a trading floor is a professional environment. Most people who are hyper-aggressive and bully other traders on the desk, or live the party lifestyle, are eventually shown the door. A lot of people are fighting to get a seat at a trading desk, and if a trader doesn't perform exceptionally or behave appropriately that seat will quickly become available to someone else. Huge sums of money are at stake and firms are not interested in making accommodations.

Like in any profession, a few bad apples can produce a negative stereotype for anyone engaged in the same line of work. Yes, there are Ferrari-driving, fast-living individuals, but these aren't representative of the majority of traders, and certainly not the profile of someone who lasts in the business. Trading requires 100 percent dedication. Contrary to what most people outside the industry believe, the responsibilities of the job don't end when the market closes. If a major geopolitical event happens on a Saturday, a trader can't afford to wait until Monday morning to think about its implications for the markets. On Sunday night, a diligent trader is checking to see how the overseas markets are opening, and the end of the workday on Friday means already digging into the voluminous amount of reading required to effectively prepare for the week ahead.

What I've observed over the years is a business that is increasingly professional and less fraternal. The antics and male chauvinism going on at banks twenty years ago are no longer tolerated. This doesn't mean traders lack personality and trading floors are no-fun zones. The occasional practical joke still happens, but it's more tasteful than distasteful, a sideshow instead of the main event. Firms today are more diverse, and the traders are more refined and sophisticated, partly because they're under such intense scrutiny, but also because financial institutions have an interest in recruiting highly educated overachievers to stay competitive. There's less of a need for the former college quarterback who can network but has little knowledge of the markets.

Recruiting traders and mentoring new entrants into the field have been responsibilities I've enjoyed over the latter half of my hedge fund career. Unfortunately, many young people contemplating a career in trading believe the stereotypes surrounding the world of finance. As a result, when the chance comes to pursue a career in the industry, they're not equipped with the right mindset or tools to succeed. Putting yourself in a position to secure that first trading role will take effort and talent, and landing a job doesn't guarantee success. Realize that years of solid work, education, and training lay ahead if you've any hope of building a lasting career.

Besides, there are places for a trading career beyond Wall Street, or the "sell-side." Sell-side firms are the large investment banks and commercial banks that compete to win the investment and trading flows of institutional and retail investors. The financial industry has ballooned over the last twenty years, and the term "Wall Street" is no longer narrowly defined as the financial dealings that take place in downtown Manhattan. There is, in other words, more to Wall Street than Goldman Sachs and J.P. Morgan. Today, tens of thousands of institutions, of all sizes, across the globe are involved in the business of investing and trading. These organizations are collectively called the "buy-side."

Movies promote the image of Wall Street trading floors the size of football fields. These sell-side behemoths are not the norm. The buy-side of the industry consists of mutual funds, public and private pension funds, university endowments, charitable foundations, sovereign wealth funds, insurance companies, private equity enterprises, wealth management businesses, and hedge funds—institutions that often exist far from New York and London and aren't nearly as immense or intimidating.

While we're dispelling common misconceptions about the industry, it's important to appreciate that there's no single definition of what constitutes a trader. Broadly speaking, traders can be grouped into three categories: execution, market makers, and discretionary. Their roles are quite different from one another.

An execution trader doesn't decide WHAT to buy or sell, but rather determines the HOW, WHEN, WHERE, and with WHOM to do the trade. They're the builders in an architect/builder relationship with control over the process, but not over the end product.

Similarly, market makers also don't decide what to buy or sell. Their role is to determine the level at which they're willing to transact with clients of the firm for which they work. A market maker is like a sports bookie, ready to provide prices for anybody who wants to bet, while adjusting the odds to regulate the flow of business and limit exposure to any one outcome.

This book will specifically focus on discretionary trading, sometimes referred to as proprietary or prop trading. It's where traders have complete discretion over all decisions. A discretionary dealer doesn't set prices for clients or wait for someone to bark out an order. They can stare at their monitors all day long and not place a trade, or they can complete hundreds of trades before lunch. Because of this greater freedom of choice, discretionary traders must be highly creative and have a strong appetite for risk.

Due to regulatory changes after the financial crisis that began in 2008, discretionary trading has migrated away from sell-side firms. Owing to the "Volcker Rule," part of the Dodd-Frank legislation passed by Congress in 2010, the large banks, which once dominated proprietary trading, are now prohibited from the activity. Risk taking has been largely curtailed, even if these banks still push the limits of what is considered proprietary trading. In response, prop traders have moved to buy-side firms, which aren't subjected to the same regulatory rules.

So, where have all these talented prop traders gone to practice their craft? The most coveted prop-trading opportunity on the buy-side is at a hedge fund.

Traders choose hedge funds because they want to work in a lucrative, dynamic, and innovative setting. In this case, many of the conceptions are accurate. The advantages are immense. Hedge fund traders, as opposed to dealers at other asset management organizations, have the ability to earn performance fees, which are upwards of 20 percent of the returns. More than any other part of the industry, hedge funds are in the greatest position to benefit from breakthroughs in trading, like high-speed computing, big data analytics, and electronic execution. They're consistently the earliest adopters of new technologies, rapidly producing specialists who can exploit innovative trading practices, staying a step ahead of the competition. People are attracted to this idea of hedge funds as the pioneers of the investment world.

The flexibility of hedge funds also entices young people looking to break into the investment world. The history of hedge funds, after all, is a history of investors seeking independence from institutional rules and government regulations. They began operating in the late 1970s when traders and investors felt too constrained in their ability to trade markets at the banks. There were too many rules about the types of investments they were allowed to make and the amount of leverage they were permitted to use. Equity investors were benchmarked to the S&P 500 and bond investors to the Barclays aggregate index. Hedge funds, which are typically private partnerships, liberated these investors by giving them *carte blanche* to go after the best ideas with few restrictions. At first, the hedge fund world was a small group of unknown partnerships, many of them operating out of small offices with nothing more than a Bloomberg terminal and a couple of computer monitors. Changes in compensation, technology, regulation, and competition, however, have combined to expand it into a sophisticated $3 trillion industry with over ten thousand firms.

While all these advantages are certainly attractive, someone considering a hedge fund career must first recognize that trading roles vary dramatically from place to place.

No two hedge funds are alike. They come in all shapes and sizes, each one with its own unique culture and business model. One firm can have an investment horizon of five years, while another can have one of five seconds. Companies can specialize in numerous strategies, including long/short equity, market neutral, merger arbitrage, convertible arbitrage, event-driven, credit, distressed credit, fixed-income arbitrage, systematic, global macro, or short only. These strategies range in nature from low risk, low volatility to high risk, high volatility.

The required skills and career paths vary depending on where and what one wants to trade. The hard skills required of a trader at a distressed credit fund will be different from a trader at a non-discretionary, quant-driven hedge fund, even if there is significant overlap when it comes to the soft skills necessary for success.

Although my background is in fixed-income arbitrage, market neutral, and credit strategies, most of the observations and advice in this book are equally applicable to other areas of hedge fund trading. Most trading experiences, whether you want to trade equities, bonds, foreign exchange, or commodities in either cash or derivative format, have many similarities. The prospect of losing money, whether through trading government bonds or shares of Google, is always emotionally taxing.

The hedge fund industry has gone through significant changes, since I entered the business in 1998. As the industry grew, hedge funds lost some flexibility because of demands imposed on them by sophisticated investors, who no longer gave them free rein to pursue any strategy they chose. These investors wanted a fund to focus on a particular niche, expertise, or style of trading. They allocated to dozens of funds in an effort to manage risk through diversification. Changing the directive of the fund, or funds, has a domino effect of tampering with the investor's portfolio, a consequence many investors will not tolerate. This means it's imperative for a new entrant to find a hedge fund with a specialization suited to his or her skills and personality.

At the end of the day, hedge funds are a challenging environment, especially for someone new to finance. For starters, hedge fund operators aim to deliver absolute, not relative, performance. Traders are expected to perform consistently in both rising and falling markets. Anything less, and they may end up without a seat. Compare this to other asset management firms, where keeping pace with the market is usually sufficient, meaning greater job security and more time for an inexperienced trader to hone his or her craft.

A hedge fund trading floor has a more cutthroat atmosphere than most other investment management companies. It attracts competitive people who are content with working in a meritocratic, less secure position. They're extremely ambitious people who want to advance quickly and are, therefore, more aggressive about performing at a high level and earning money. They certainly don't shy away from risk.

There's also more of an entrepreneurial spirit on the trading floors of hedge funds, which are designed and equipped to engage new business or market opportunities whenever they arise. Insurance companies, on the other hand, stick to the same script year after year. How they're allowed to use their capital is heavily regulated.

One of my hedge fund colleagues loves to tell the story of an early experience working at a sell-side firm. Armed with fantastic trade ideas, he went to visit a large insurance company with the goal of helping it outperform its investment benchmark.

"Look, son," one of the executives told him. "I'm not paid to beat the market. I'm paid to match the market."

That tells you something about the risk-taking capacity at insurance companies.

The same is true for pension funds and many other asset management businesses. Any decision to significantly alter a strategy or shift allocations is made at a committee level or presented in front of a board of trustees at a quarterly meeting. Maybe they'll choose to move ahead, or maybe they'll simply agree to do further research and revisit the idea three months later at the next meeting, at which point the opportunity may have come and gone. Major decisions at hedge funds can be made in a matter of hours or even minutes.

Nevertheless, whatever type of trading you take up, whether it's in the equity, bond, commodity, credit, or foreign exchange market, and whether you do it on the sell-side or the buy-side, there's no escaping the fact that you'll need certain talents, knowledge, and a personality to match.

Strong communication skills, an appreciation of behavioral biases like risk aversion and overconfidence, the ability to control your emotions, a strong quantitative background, and an openness to learning from mistakes are only some of the attributes that help traders succeed in this business. If you're considering a future in hedge fund trading, this book will teach you how to identify and acquire the hard and soft skills needed to land the right position on the proper trading desk, so you can increase the odds of shaping a satisfying and lucrative career in the industry.

This book will help you facilitate an honest self-assessment to determine if trading at a hedge fund is right for you, increasing the odds that you'll find success and not end up as a candidate for rejection, failure, or burnout. If you believe hedge fund trading is your calling, this book will reveal how to gain an edge on the tens of thousands of other applicants with similar hopes.

It will also guide you through the early stages of working at a hedge fund, providing insights on what to expect and what is expected of you. I've seen many talented individuals sail through the hiring process, only to commit career-ending mistakes shortly after the opening bell of their careers.

Success isn't achieved overnight, or once you find a spot on a trading desk. Developing into a good trader takes years. It's a craft that is both art and science. The science portion of the equation is becoming more pronounced in recent years with an ever-increasing demand for applicants with strong quantitative, math, and statistical abilities. The artful element, the part of the occupation that requires a trader to have control over his or her emotions, effective communication skills, and an ability to manage risk and loss, is as important as ever.

A dynamic work environment, excellent pay, and objective feedback make trading a rewarding career. It's a profession, though, that comes with stress, high industry turnover, and demanding hours. If you're entering the industry expecting a *Wolf of Wall Street* type lifestyle, you'll most likely be disappointed. Instead, prepare yourself to be asleep by nine most evenings so you can be up before the crack of dawn. Understand that a trading career requires a lifetime of learning that starts the moment you set your sights on this path, and it will take years before you achieve proficiency. Don't allow early, needless missteps to derail you from achieving your dream of becoming a successful hedge fund trader.

SECTION I

GETTING IN

CHAPTER ONE

FINDING YOUR PATH TO SUCCESS

I had made it. After months of interviews and tests, I, along with a hundred other future traders, sat in a presentation room waiting for the first day of the Merrill Lynch training program to commence. It was day one of what was guaranteed to be a successful and lucrative career—I was convinced—an attitude that was surely floating through the heads of the hundred or so other trainees. The chosen few from a group of close to ten thousand applicants, we were young and smart, and nothing was going to stop us from conquering the world of finance.

Minutes later, a senior managing director opened the training session. After welcoming us to the firm, he asked us to take a quick glance at our fellow colleagues filling the room.

"Fifty percent of you," he declared, "will be gone in five years; 90 percent of you will be gone in ten." Then, he shared a nugget of advice. "Every morning, when you wake up, you better come into the office ready to bite the ass off a bear."

The managing director's statistics did nothing to knock the confidence out of us. Everyone in the room—including me—assumed that it was the next guy who would end up a casualty. We lacked the maturity to understand that the numbers applied to every single one of us. Failure, for most in the room, was a foreign concept. Chronic over-achievers for most of our lives—which was the reason we were called to sit in the conference room that day—we saw no reason why a long history of success should suddenly stop at this current station.

However, the stats don't lie. In twenty-plus years in the industry, I've witnessed, firsthand, this considerable attrition rate. Most people do in fact leave the trading world after a short period of time, and few survive past year ten. Longevity and stability aren't hallmarks of a career in trading.

WHY IS ATTRITION SO HIGH?

Massive trader attrition exists for multiple reasons, and some are the same factors impacting attrition rates in other industries.

The most common reason why people leave the business is simple: they shouldn't have joined in the first place. Some individuals are just not suited for the trials and tribulations of life on a trading floor.

Nobody truly knows what it's like to trade for a living until they begin doing it, so it's the obligation of the hiring firm to properly screen potential candidates. Sometimes the screening is inadequate or insufficient. Perhaps someone inside the company vouched for the candidate, or the hire dazzled the interviewer, but when the moment came to perform, he or she couldn't handle the work. Certain raw capabilities, like the ability to tolerate stress, are difficult to gauge until the trader hits the floor.

Maybe the person didn't have a suitable disposition for a trading desk. Not having the right personality doesn't mean having a bad personality. It just means having the wrong makeup for working in a tight-knit group under extraordinary pressure. Sometimes it means merely not having the right type of personality for a particular style of trading, an issue we'll explore later.

Candidates are liable to overstate their skill set during the interview process. They'll say whatever they think will land them the job. Usually, the exaggeration isn't even a conscious effort. An applicant may say he is a people person when he is really not, or the candidate may have some experience creating spreadsheets, so he or she boasts about being an expert in Excel. These are cases of the applicant failing to appreciate the difference between adequate and good, and the fault lies squarely with the firm for not doing sufficient due diligence to verify claims made by candidates.

Sometimes, a professor, family member, or friend convinces someone to pursue a trading career even though it doesn't suit his or her skill set, or he or she lacks passion or interest for the work. The person may have little sense, or a misperception, of what the day-to-day work of a trader actually entails. They're attracted to the allure of high compensation, and only after they start working do they soon realize they're not cut out for the profession.

Some skills simply don't translate well into trading. A recruit may have excelled at calculus in school and believed this was an indication that he or she would do well in the role. Though, when the person arrived at the trading floor, he or she had difficulty applying this knowledge. Moving from the theoretical academic world to the practical world of finance is hard for some people. It's one thing to be bright and finish at the top of your class, but competing under pressure when money—lots of it—is on the line is another sport altogether.

Bailing early from the industry is not uncommon. This is a costly mistake in terms of time and money, for both the trader and the firm. The employer loses the potential to hire a more suitable person for the position. It is expensive in terms of time to train and develop a new hire to the point where he or she can add value to the firm. If somebody leaves shortly after training, it is costly to the firm. They have to start from the beginning with a new hire. The recruit also misses a chance to find a more fitting role elsewhere. Trading takes a tremendous amount of commitment and focus. It can be a brutal atmosphere. Without passion and interest for the work, a trader will never survive.

Obviously, it's challenging to ascertain all of this information about candidates before they start working. That is why many companies run potential hires through numerous interviews with multiple people in several formats. The hiring process isn't perfect, and businesses are constantly looking for ways to minimize these types of hiring mistakes.

The errors mentioned above are responsible for high levels of attrition through the first few years in the role. Burnout, on the other hand, is a reason traders leave the profession during the five-to-ten-year mark. The long hours, the pressure to continually perform, and the stress of losing substantial amounts of money make trading an extremely demanding occupation.

Some folks cannot handle the constant feedback. Minutes, or sometimes seconds after a trade is executed, a trader can see whether it was a success or failure. He will pat himself on the back, or he will start questioning what went wrong. Compare this to most industries where performance reviews happen on an annual basis.

Contributing to the possibility of burnout is the tremendous toll trading takes on one's physical well-being. On trading floors, there are no hour-long lunch breaks, and you're sitting down for the majority of the day. A trading assistant will fetch sandwiches from a local restaurant, and the crew will either wolf them down at their desks in a matter of minutes, or take periodic bites throughout the remainder of the day. Going to the gym takes commitment, because either the trader works out at an ungodly hour in the morning before trading hours begin, or after work when there's little left—physically or mentally—in the tank. Most traders choose convenience over health, which means no gym and usually a hamburger and fries for lunch. Firms, increasingly aware of the issue, are beginning to encourage healthier living by attaching fitness rooms and healthy cafeterias to their offices.

Stress relief on a trading floor is a sport in its own right. Humor and good-natured competition rank high among the remedies. Combined, they form unparalleled entertainment. On the large trading floors, for example, eating contests have always served as a great distraction from market stress. Some dealing floors occasionally turn into giant dodgeball arenas with traders battling the salespeople. (Foam balls of course...usually.)

For a significant number of individuals, such juvenile trading floor antics aren't enough to blow off all the steam, and those who lack an outlet for the stress often end up falling victim to attrition.

Bad performance is another cause for early exits. In an industry where a person's function is to generate trading profits, it becomes apparent, sooner rather than later, whether the person is performing. The feedback is immediate and indisputable—the numbers don't lie. This isn't figure skating where two judges may have vastly disparate opinions on a skater's musical interpretation. In trading, there's a highly objective evaluation—the P&L (Profit and Loss) statement—and it's calculated every minute of every day. Trading performance is the primary driver of one's ability to stay and advance at a firm. While certain qualitative metrics are also evaluated, like whether the person is a team player, is reliable, and brings a good attitude to the desk, the ultimate measure of success is numerical. Many people are unable to handle this daily pressure.

Numerical performance isn't the only indicator of underperformance. Junior traders and trading assistants may not have their own P&L, yet they are judged with equal scrutiny. The role of these team members is to add value to the desk by making the head trader's life easier. If they're having difficulty moving up the learning curve, possess a bad attitude, are unlikable, or have lost the boss's trust, then they won't advance and will possibly be forced off the floor.

At the end of each year, Goldman Sachs is known to go through a formal process of firing those deemed to be in the bottom five-to-ten percent of its staff. Employees are thoroughly evaluated by everybody they deal with in the organization and are ranked according to these scores. This process (which some refer to as "Rank and Yank") helps identify star performers, but it's also used to identify the weakest employees. Jack Welch conducted a similar assessment at GE through what he called a "Vitality Curve." Many hedge funds may not have a formal process in place, but most will regularly replace chronically underperforming traders with less expensive, comparable talent.

Confidence—knowing what you know—is key to becoming a successful trader and avoiding attrition. Equally crucial, however, is acknowledging what you don't know. Many assistants come into the position with a degree of arrogance and believe they should be trading from day one. They find it insulting to fetch lunch for the desk and perform routine calculations. They need to accept, not resent, the need to earn respect and responsibility.

If you're unwilling to learn or don't accept the normal training protocols, and instead walk around with a stubborn attitude, telling anyone who will listen how you can run the organization better than the people in charge, then your days in the industry will be numbered.

SOMETIMES IT'S NOT IN YOUR HANDS

Like many other industries, the trading business is cyclical. When times are good and the market is up, trading desks generally do well. Firms swell in size as they hire to keep up with growth. On the flip side, when the economy is suffering and trading desks are missing their numbers, cost cutting turns fierce. People are the most expensive line item in the cost structure, and the layoffs come quickly.

Senior and established personnel are, more often than not, the first to go. Every managing director or senior partner who is cut loose provides enough savings to keep multiple junior members on the team.

Occasionally, entire desks are banished from the company. A fixed-income division, for example, can take up an entire floor of a large building, but there can be several sectors within the broader fixed income business—mortgage, treasury, municipal, credit, swaps, options. At any point, but especially during harder periods, a firm may conduct a broad evaluation of the trading desk and conclude that a particular sector—say mortgages—isn't generating a sufficient return. The company abandons that product and suddenly, the whole team is out of work.

Industry consolidation has increased in recent years as companies look to cut costs to maintain their competitiveness. This is true both on the sell-side and the buy-side. The burdens of compliance on the sell-side and fee compression on the buy-side are too overwhelming for smaller banks and investment firms to bear. Mergers and acquisitions (M&A), therefore, are a regular feature of the finance industry. As mentioned, compensation is by far the largest expense item, and it's through massive layoffs that firms can achieve cost savings. Even though the purpose of consolidation is to extract efficiencies and economies of scale, they aren't always executed in the most thoughtful manner.

I was working at UBS in the late 1990s when it merged with Swiss Bank Corporation. These were two massive global banks with tens of thousands of employees. Despite the freedom to pick the best employees from both enterprises, little attempt was made to identify the best performers from either bank. Instead, the decision makers focused on the question of which businesses from each bank were worth maintaining. Deciding to keep the fixed-income division of Swiss Bank Corporation meant that thousands of people at UBS were set to lose their spots. This choice came down to politics, not merit. The fixed-income unit at Swiss Bank didn't perform better than the UBS team. Rather, the decision makers wanted to protect the head of the division at Swiss bank, and along with it, the hundreds of other people underneath him. In other words, you can be vulnerable in an M&A scenario regardless of your performance.

Some people fired after a merger or acquisition will look for, and find, a position at a competing firm. But, with greater consolidation and less costly workers regularly entering the industry, there are fewer openings. Obviously, laggards who have historically underperformed will have a more significant challenge latching on to a new employer, and older workers, whose wages have steadily increased over the years, may price themselves out of the market.

Firms do fail. Hedge funds open and close every day. As in any business, a substantial number of new entrants don't survive more than a few years. Moreover, according to HFR, a leading hedge fund research company, the average annual return in their HFRI Index was just 3.4 percent from 2006 to 2016.[1] Performance fees constitute the majority of profits for most hedge funds, but if there's no performance, then there are no fees. In a down year, the traders may not receive a bonus. Many times, the management fees accrued during these down periods isn't enough to keep the business running, and the fund management company closes its doors. This factor makes a career in trading risky, especially if the trader is joining a less-established firm.

SELF-ASSESSMENT IS KEY

Some reasons for the high level of attrition are beyond one's control. Still, a good portion of the attrition is because people make the wrong choice and enter an industry that isn't the right fit for their personalities. This is a career that has biases toward certain character

---

[1]   Nir Kaissar, "Hedge Funds Have a Performance Problem," March 24, 2016, https://www.bloomberg.com/gadfly/articles/2016-03-24/hedge-funds-have-a-performance-problem.

traits. For example, people who have trouble accepting and incorporating feedback or have difficulty regrouping after setbacks will not excel on a trading desk. Through gaining a clearer picture of your personality and examining it through clear and honest eyes, you can speculate whether your disposition is right for this industry. An honest self-assessment, therefore, is crucial if you're considering a trading career.

How do you conduct a proper self-assessment? First, gain an accurate understanding of what the job entails, which is the main purpose of this book. Next, take a comprehensive personality test, so you can see whether you possess the basic requirements and skills for success. I'd recommend the NEO-AC personality test.

The NEO-AC test evaluates five major personality factors: Neuroticism, Extraversion, Openness, Agreeableness, and Conscientiousness. Each factor has six subordinate traits that are graded as well. Neuroticism, for example, has anxiety and impulsiveness as subordinate traits. Trust and altruism are subordinate traits of agreeableness. This means the test subject is scored on thirty different personality factors.

A respected psychiatrist, Dr. Jason Williams, along with his father, Larry Williams, a veteran futures trader and systems developer, administered the NEO-AC test to some of the world's most prosperous traders. A list of how they scored on the various factors is published in Dr. Jason Williams's book, *The Mental Edge in Trading*, and the results provide valuable insights into the minds of highly successful operators.

The test, which must be administered by a licensed psychologist or psychiatrist and takes no more than an hour to complete, allows you to see how your temperament matches up against some of the industry's titans. From this comparison, you can learn not only if a future in trading is right for you, but also which specific area of the industry aligns best with your personality.

Research shows personalities are mostly fixed and unalterable. It's better, therefore, to get insightful feedback before you waste everyone's time going down the wrong road. If you crumble under pressure, don't expect the trading floor to be a training ground to build up your tolerance. You either have the temperment or you don't.

I have taken the NEO-AC test myself and found the results to be broadly consistent with my behavior as a trader. Having done many styles of trading throughout my career, I can tell you I'm more suited to certain styles of trading because of my personality. Let me be frank:

I don't consider myself a good short-term directional trader. Making bets on whether the market—stocks, bonds, or commodities—will rise or fall, necessitates low levels of anxiety—one of the sub-categories measured in the NEO-AC. Sure enough, my personal anxiety score was considered merely average when compared to the general population. The most successful directional traders in Williams's study had very low scores in the anxiety subcategory.

Relative value trading—my personal area of focus—is generally associated with a lower level of price volatility and a longer trade horizon. Lower volatility forms of trading don't test tolerance for anxiety in the same way as high volatility strategies, which is why it has proven to be more suitable to my personality. I'm not suggesting relative value trading is without risk—far from it. It's just a different type of risk and requires a different temperament.

Part of the evolution a trader undergoes is discovering the trading style that agrees with his or her behavior and qualities. The subcategories of the NEO-AC will help provide some of these insights. People who are seriously considering a career in trading should take the test and have the results evaluated by a licensed psychologist who's aware of the daily stresses on a trading floor. Additionally, taking a test like this prior to applying for jobs in the industry can provide interesting material to discuss in an interview.

The task of a trader is challenging enough. If you discover through the test that your personality is ideal for directional trading and you choose to look for a job as a relative value specialist, you're not optimizing your chances of success. In my years in the industry, I've observed that the people who are still working after the ten-year mark are traders who have found styles of trading consistent with their personalities.

There are two ways to find your comfort zone. One approach is to engage in a serious self-assessment before you begin trading, as discussed above. Trial and error is the other way to uncover your ideal situation. This was how I found my way in the trading world, as I didn't take the NEO-AC test until much later in my career. I wouldn't recommend others rely on trial and error. One of the worst things you can do is put considerable effort into becoming a trader, and then fail because you chose the wrong type of trading. You cost yourself time and your firm money and, in a constantly consolidating business, a second chance is never guaranteed. Failure can also play havoc with your self-confidence. You may misinterpret negative feedback as a sign you're not destined for success, when in reality, it may be that you were simply not the right fit for a certain style.

Part of any self-assessment should be asking yourself some tough questions about your ability to adapt to the hedge fund industry's unique culture. Reflect on your motives for entering the business. If you see trading as just a job or a quick way to earn some easy money, working at a hedge fund is not right for you. It's a full-time endeavor, a way of life. The education is ongoing and unrelenting, and if trading isn't your passion, you'll lack the motivation to devote the years needed to become well-rounded. If you'll be spending fourteen-hour days at the office, don't you owe it to yourself to do what you love?

Next, are you comfortable in a fast-paced environment? On the trading floor, new information comes at lightning speed, whether it's market volatility or geopolitical developments. Witness the constant barrage of "intelligence" relayed on networks like Bloomberg and CNBC. If you find such flows of facts and figures overwhelming and you have difficulty sorting out the pertinent data from the noise, then this isn't a good career choice for you.

Take Payroll Friday, for example. At 8:29 on the first Friday of every month, you can hear a pin drop on a trading floor, but when the clock strikes half-past the hour, all hell breaks loose. Markets begin to jump and gyrate, lighting up the computer monitors. Markets have already started to react, regardless of whether the employment numbers are high or low, and there's a stream of information to absorb, which takes us to the next question.

Do you possess the confidence to make quick decisions with limited information at your disposal? You'll be forced to quickly process economic data like the employment numbers. You don't have time to do a thorough analysis of the many implications an above- or below-consensus number has for the market you're trading. You have to decide what to do without the luxury of consulting others. The information is incomplete, contradictory, and confusing. You don't have the option of taking a pass. Following your instinct and established process is the only path forward.

Some people cannot operate in this situation. They're too analytical or never feel an investigation is complete. Decisions paralyze them. These people may make excellent analysts, but not traders. In trading, abstaining from a decision is a decision in itself. Besides, having all the information in trading means all the relevant knowledge is already out there and the opportunity has passed.

Still interested in a hedge fund career? You'll need to get comfortable with the precarious nature of the hedge fund industry. You have limited control over the performance of your employer, and therefore, limited control over your job security. Even if you're profitable, your firm can still fold because of the lackluster returns of your colleagues. Moreover, markets, in the end, are uncertain. Even if you and your colleagues are capable, your trading results will always be uncertain. This isn't the right profession if you need to know in concrete terms how your career will unfold regarding advancement and earning power.

Finally, are you comfortable taking risks? The task, at its essence, is to assess risk. Gamblers, however, need not apply. Risks are calculated by estimating the values of certain outcomes. A trader is always weighing the probability of winning, and the size of the gain, versus the likelihood of losing money and the size of the potential loss. Risk cannot be avoided, but it always needs to be managed.

People who are totally averse to risk need not apply, either. Like many of the qualities listed above, it's about assessing whether you have the right balance, in this case between brazenness and cautiousness. Risk avoidance, as we will see in a later chapter, can be equally destructive to a trading career as excessive risk taking.

The goal of listing these potential pitfalls isn't to discourage anybody from pursuing a career in trading. Rather, I wish somebody had sat me down at the start of university

A DAY IN THE LIFE OF A HEDGE FUND TRADER

6:00 a.m.: Wake up. No alarm needed. Grab the iPad by the bed to quickly check overnight market moves.

7:00 a.m.: Arrive at the office. Execute a detailed scan of the information displayed on one of the four large-screen monitors.

8:30 a.m.–4:30 p.m.: Remain glued to the desk. Talk on the phone, watch the markets, execute trades, and read research.

4:30 p.m.: Start returning phone calls that came in during the trading session. Begin reviewing the P&L for the day.

9:00 p.m.–10:30 p.m.: Read market recaps, research, and emails, while listening to Bloomberg TV's analysis of the Tokyo market open.

11:00 p.m.: Crash. Hard.

and told me about the sacrifices I'd have to make to successfully navigate medical school and what the day-to-day life of a doctor was truly like. Eventually, I figured this out on my own after wasting a few precious years. A trading career can be full of rewards, but you need to know what you're getting yourself into, and the sooner the better.

I'VE GOT THE GOODS, NOW HOW DO I GET IN?

The typical path to becoming a trader has evolved from the time I broke into the industry in the mid-1990s. There weren't many hedge funds and most people interested in trading coveted a position at one of the bulge bracket firms on Wall Street. Back then it was mainly about connections. You needed to know people in the industry, maybe a relative or family friend who held a senior position in a firm and could get an application in front of the hiring committee. The big banks would target a group of twenty elite schools, usually the alma maters of current senior employees. Getting through the door was significantly more challenging for anyone who was not a student at those select schools.

Nevertheless, applicants still had to demonstrate a specific set of qualifications once they got a foot in the door. Most of these applicants had honors or graduate degrees in finance or economics from Ivy League-caliber schools. Candidates generally had a strong comprehension of markets and above average quant skills. Possessing strong personal skills was also vital, since the industry remained somewhat of an old boys' club.

Nowadays, the path to achieving a seat at a trading desk incorporates the startling ways technology has advanced and altered the industry. Through the use of algorithms, companies like Goldman Sachs have a greater ability to locate and recruit the most qualified candidates in the world. The firm is using technology to scan résumés for certain words and experiences it believes are good barometers of a person's success. This means the firm is no longer limited to recruiting from top tier schools. They cast their nets out wide, opening up the application process to hundreds of schools in hopes of discovering diamonds in the rough. In other words, no need to find us, we'll find you. The algorithms allow them to easily weed out unqualified candidates. They can pre-screen applicants and cut down on some of the inherent inefficiencies that come with hiring people through connections.

Educationally speaking, quant-heavy degrees like computer science and engineering are more favored than general finance and economics. Having passable quantitative skills is no longer satisfactory. Advanced knowledge of software, computing, and databases are expected from all prospective employees. Raw quant skills are more imperative than an understanding of the markets, because the former are skills much harder to acquire after you've entered the business, whereas the latter can be taught, assuming there's a foundation to build on. New entrants should be critically aware of this change in the industry.

DO YOU HAVE THE CHARACTER AND INTEGRITY TO TRADE?

Character and integrity as requirements in trading? Most people would think that sounds like a bad joke, but unless you're going to trade your own money exclusively, these traits matter a great deal. If you manage other people's money, which is the main goal of most hedge funds and other asset managers, character and integrity now matter more than ever. In an age when reputation is absolutely critical, recruiters have grown extremely cautious about hiring individuals who have any record of poor judgment. If they spot anything dishonest about the résumé, even an embellishment, they'll pass on the candidate.

In 2012, I attended the CNBC Delivering Alpha Conference in New York, where Jim Cramer interviewed Preet Bharara, the well-known former US Attorney for the Southern District of New York. People, Bharara remarked, usually enter the industry with a misguided outlook. They assume that because the competition is fierce, employers want applicants who show a willingness to push the rules right up to the edge. New entrants to the business are always asking him how close to the line they can get without crossing it. That is the wrong question to ask. A firm shouldn't want to hire anyone with such a mentality, Bharara argues, since it's precisely people who deal in these gray zones that raise suspicions of impropriety and could earn a phone call from the US attorney's office. When that happens, investors get nervous and redeem their capital, even if the line was never crossed. It takes mere suspicion, not formal charges, to upend a firm's reputation.

Compared to the pre-financial crisis period, hedge funds now operate in a much tougher regulatory environment. Beginning in 2011, new rules under the Dodd-Frank regulation required private funds with more than $100 million in assets to register with the SEC. Under SEC regulation, firms are routinely examined for compliance deficiencies. Companies that don't meet SEC standards can face significant fines. The willingness of financial regulators to pursue financial improprieties, fueled by some high-profile, successful prosecutions, has put hedge funds on high alert when it comes to following the letter and the spirit of the law. Hedge fund partnerships have responded by institutionalizing compliance procedures. They have low tolerance for employees who don't take these rules seriously.

The SEC is the official watchdog, but it's not the only group of people carefully monitoring the inner workings of hedge funds. In fact, investors are probably the greatest driver for enhanced compliance. Hedge funds, after all, aren't raising money from the average person. They're targeting institutions like pension funds, endowments, and sovereign wealth funds, which have multiple options of where to invest their money and greater resources to do proper due diligence. Call it the "Madoff effect."

Attracting clients is harder than ever. An excellent track record is, of course, an essential metric when they are making this decision, and twenty years ago potential investors could narrow their choices to a handful of high-performing management companies. With the industry's tremendous growth came the ability to now choose from hundreds of well-performing funds. To narrow their choices, these investors hire consultants and private investigators to perform a complete forensic analysis, not just on strategy and performance, but also on the firm's internal operating and compliance procedures, searching for anything that may be perceived as untoward or a conflict of interest. From a "CYA," or a cover your ass perspective, half of the prospects are eliminated, because they don't have squeaky-clean operations. Consultants have a letter grade for the firms they analyze on behalf of investors, and a low grade will provide an excuse for allocators to move on and evaluate the next one on the list. Running a spotless operation has become a good business practice. Companies won't jeopardize potential business by hiring someone with an indecent personality or past.

When potential investors vet my shop, standard procedure calls on each of the other principals and me to provide our social security numbers so consultants can run thorough background checks. They will dig deep, examining political donations, any civil or criminal cases—both past and present—along with company affiliations and employment histories.

More than twenty-five years ago in the summer before starting my MBA, I took over a friend's painting company as he gallivanted through Europe. The entire gig lasted three months, but twenty-five years later, this friend got a call from an investigator wanting to know about my work at the company, and why I'd left. This summer stint wasn't exactly listed under "Work Experience" on my resume, yet the consultants uncovered it. To this day, I have no idea how they found out. Fortunately, my buddy didn't have anything bad to say!

Investors look for reasons to say "no" to an investment and not for evidence to say "yes." Any strike against the firm, no matter how small, is enough to remove it from the final list of two or three hedge funds.

Hedge funds will do everything in their power to avoid suggestions of impropriety. In some instances, cameras record every inch of office space. All communications—phone calls and emails—are monitored and recorded. Access to non-company email may be forbidden. Political donations and personal trading must be preapproved and logged. A detailed list of personal investments must be disclosed and updated annually. Firms go as far as blocking access to social media to avoid a situation where an employee mistakenly releases inside information.

Does every hedge fund take integrity and character into consideration when hiring new employees? Of course not. While hedge funds may not hire someone with a known checkered past, not all enterprises may put forth an adequate effort to investigate candidates' backgrounds. Further, there will always be businesses that prioritize profits over character. These are the companies you should avoid when possible. If you work at a firm involved in an ethical or legal scandal, your own reputation can be tarnished—even if you had zero connection to the allegation. Companies that take a long-term view appreciate the importance of avoiding damage to their reputation and will pass on any employment candidate who brings with them such risk, even if it's only guilt by association.

SELF-ASSESSMENT IS NOT ENOUGH

A solid, honest self-assessment is not the final step before looking for a job. It's just the beginning. The competition to get into the industry is fierce, and you'll need an edge greater than knowing why you want to go into the industry and the kind of desk you want to sit at.

In the early 1990s, in the midst of weak economic activity, I tried to land my first trading opportunity. Soon, I realized I didn't have the necessary requirements to even land an interview. I wasn't standing out in any way, and my résumé was going straight to the shredder. A self-assessment directed me to a specific area of finance, but it also highlighted certain deficiencies in the "package" I could offer potential employers. I was missing essential skills, and the ones I possessed were no better than those of the majority of other candidates. Obtaining the skills needed to get into the industry, as you'll read in the next chapter, is a job in itself.

CHAPTER TWO

THE TOP 20 PERCENT RULE AND ITS LIMITS

"Dear Mr. Friesen, Thank you for your interest in First National Bank of Springfield. After careful consideration of your résumé, we have determined there is no position that fits your particular skill set at the present time. We will contact you should that change in the future. We offer our best wishes for success as you pursue your career goals. With deepest regrets..."

Mildly disappointing, but it was the first response I'd received. I tried to stay optimistic. Hundreds of cover letters and résumés were still waiting to be answered (this was before email and LinkedIn). Going in, I knew it was a low-percentage game. After all, I employed a somewhat pie-in-the-sky strategy of responding to advertisements or writing managers unsolicited, knowing all I needed was one positive response. Besides, this was not a total rejection, and maybe, as the letter implied, it was just a matter of this particular bank not being the right fit.

A few more letters came over the next several weeks. They all carried the same inoffensive tone and positive message. Soon it became painfully obvious that these were nothing more than form responses, or what are affectionately known as FOAD (Fuck Off And Die) letters.

Staring at the collage of FOAD letters I'd assembled on my dorm room wall motivated me to keep plugging away. I researched more firms—again, without the Internet—and prepared more inquiries. Several more months passed and eventually, I ran out of room on the wall. I must have had more than fifty rejection letters pinned up as high as the ceiling. I was clueless as to what I was doing wrong. In my mind, getting a job should have been a breeze. Why wasn't it enough to be a good candidate who desperately wanted a shot, worked hard, did my research, and could craft a convincing cover letter without typos?

Years earlier, my father had given me advice before starting boarding school: "Don't kill yourself trying to be number one. Just make sure you finish in the top 20 percent." His theory, developed through his personal experience, was that a person didn't close many doors of opportunities if he or she were consistently evaluated in the top quintile relative to the person's peers. This was true, he believed, in school, work, sports, and every other area of life. Once you've made it into the top 20 percent, other factors would determine your success.

It was my father's 20 percent rule that was preventing me from getting my first break in the industry. The reality stung. Maybe I had the passion and the work ethic, but I lacked some crucial requirements. In several critical areas, I ranked far below the top 20 percent of the applicant pool, meaning I couldn't make it through the first screening of candidates. If I couldn't pass the initial screening, I'd never get invited for an interview, and it's pretty difficult to secure a spot if nobody will even speak to you.

In the investment banking and trading sectors, the applicant pool is unusually large, and few job seekers ultimately receive offers. Morgan Stanley had approximately 90,000 applications for its analyst and associates summer internship program in 2013. Only 1,000 aspirants received offers, which is less than 2 percent. Goldman Sachs is also estimated to accept fewer than 2 percent of applicants. Other banks, like J.P. Morgan and Citibank are slightly more accepting with rates hovering just under 3 percent.[1] Compare those numbers to Harvard, where a little over 5 percent of candidates were accepted into the class of 2019. You could say that landing an internship on Wall Street is more challenging than gaining admission into an Ivy League school.

Hedge funds don't publish their hiring data, but suffice it to say it's even harder to land a spot at a hedge fund straight out of school. Some offer internships, which are a fantastic way to get through the door, but many won't hire inexperienced full-time people to join their desks.

Despite the use of algorithms to target applicants, as discussed in the last chapter, candidates looking for a start on Wall Street must follow a standardized hiring process. What's changed with algorithms is the enhanced ability of employers to scan through tens of thousands of résumés and identify the candidates who meet their criteria. This technology helps employers weed out the bottom 80 percent of applicants who lack the basic requirements. If they're starting with 100,000 applicants, they're still left with 20,000 contenders after the initial screening.

Luck, of course, plays a role in securing that first assignment, but you cannot get lucky, or even compete with the

1   "Morning Coffee: Transpires It's harder to Get into Goldman Than You Thought," last modified June 6, 2016, http://news.efinancialcareers.com/uk-en/246529/percentage-of-students-accepted-by-goldman-sachs.

other candidates, unless you're in the top quintile of the pool. To be clear, every firm determines its cutoff point. It could be 30 percent, or it could be 10 percent. The key is that you need to be better than your peers. The less you leave to luck, the better.

THE BASIC REQUIREMENTS DEFINED

Inserting yourself into this top echelon of candidates will not happen overnight, and it will take work. It took me four years to get into the top 20 percent, starting with two years in a non-trading role at a small Japanese bank, followed by a two-year MBA.

Identifying the skills that firms are assessing during that initial screening will enable you to ascertain your shortcomings.

SCHOOL CHOICE AND CLASS RANKING

Unfortunately, despite the stated goal of trying to identify the best candidates from all walks of life, a degree of snobbery remains in the hiring process, and one of the first things an employer will look at on a résumé is schooling, GPA, and class ranking. Not all schools are created equal in the eyes of recruiters, who place a premium on individuals from top schools. This is a matter of efficiency, with firms essentially relying on the school's vetting process. If you're good enough for Harvard or Stanford, the thinking goes, then you may be good enough for us.

Additionally, these schools are known to be academically rigorous, so a student who manages to graduate in the top half of the class has already proven to any potential employer that he or she can handle a competitive atmosphere or swim with the big fish, so to speak. Therefore, class ranking and GPA are also critical.

The good news is you don't have to go to an Ivy League school to get hired as a trader. A firm will look favorably on you if you went to a reputable second-tier school and finished in the top quintile of the class. Attending a non-recognizable school doesn't mean you have zero chance of landing a job, but the likelihood is diminished if you're not at the top end of the class.

Personally, I don't assign too much weight to one school over another, although maybe I'd feel differently if I'd gone to Harvard. For me, what's more relevant is whether the school is considered respectable and competitive. Then next thing I'll look at is how the candidate performed at the institution.

Class ranking and GPA tells me something concrete about an applicant. If you went to Harvard and finished in the bottom quintile of the class, much of the benefit of attending such an elite institution is lost. Why would anyone gamble on a candidate who couldn't rise to the occasion and compete with the best when this is exactly what they will need to do on a trading floor?

Alternatively, an applicant who is in the top quintile of a second- or third-tier school has proven he or she can rise above his or her peers, even if it's at a lower level of difficulty. A skeptic may point out that the school isn't an Ivy League institution, but we can't be certain how the candidate would have performed in a more rigourous setting. Maybe the person had the credentials to go to an Ivy League school but chose their college for another reason, like financial aid or the need to be close to a sick relative. It's quite possible the candidate may have been in the top quintile at any school. Some people rise to the occasion when facing stiffer competition. We frequently see this in the sports world when an athlete steps up at a critical moment.

The goal is to demonstrate that you've competed and succeeded in your most recent setting, so it's imperative you pick a school where you have a reasonable chance of finishing in the top portion of your class.

In his book, *David and Goliath: Underdogs, Misfits, and the Art of Battling Giants*, Malcolm Gladwell relates a story about a young woman who wanted to become a scientist and make a difference in the world. She was accepted to Brown University, as well as University of Maryland, her safety school. Passing on an Ivy League education did not seem prudent, so she chose Brown. A graduate of an unexceptional high school, she was not fully prepared for the competitiveness of the Ivy League environment, and quickly grew frustrated by negative feedback and her inability to excel. Eventually, it became too much, and she ended up pursuing a career outside of the sciences. Gladwell hypothesizes that if this woman had accepted the offer from Maryland, a less competitive setting, she may have excelled, and the success would have encouraged her to pursue a PhD in the sciences and realize her dream. Sometimes there's an advantage to being the "big fish in a small pond."[2]

CHOOSE YOUR COURSES WISELY

A respectable class ranking at a top tier institution isn't enough. You need to take coursework that will gain you marketable skills and prove to any potential employer that you can be an asset from day one. Being in the music

---

2   "Malcolm Gladwell on the Ivy League," April 17, 2014, https://www.ivycoach.com/
    the-ivy-coach-blog/tag/malcolm-gladwell-on-the-ivy-league/.

program is interesting, and it can certainly help a résumé stand out, but a candidate should still have some basic coursework in four main categories—math, statistics, computer programming, and economics.

Quant skills have always been necessary in trading, but with the proliferation of sophisticated software, high-speed computing, and advanced programming languages, it's almost a deal breaker if a candidate lacks these skills, or, at the very least, cannot display a capability to improve them quickly. Trading is a numbers-oriented industry and math is a fundamental component of quant skills. Using complex mathematical procedures and analytics are important, but a trader must be very good at basic mental math, too. Performing quick calculations in your head is a critical skill on the trading desk.

Statistics is a second important area of knowledge. Standard deviation and probability calculations are used frequently on the trading floor. With database costs coming down and computers gaining speed, big data allows for the analysis of millions of variables simultaneously to identify correlations, probabilities, anomalies, and trends in the markets. The goal is to find meaning in data that is not apparent to the naked eye. Proprietary data analytics provide potential advantages and opportunities unidentifiable to other players in the market.

Computer programming and modeling, at all levels, are everyday activities on a trading floor. Sometimes it's building an Excel spreadsheet with graphs to track the performance of a trade, or it could be writing code for a new execution algorithm. You don't have to be an expert programmer, but you do need some basic knowledge. A deep comprehension of statistical computer languages like R and Python, as opposed to a rudimentary understanding, will set you apart as a candidate, which is exactly what you are trying to do at this stage of the process.

Even in an industry that has become quant-centric, all candidates should have a strong knowledge of economics and how fundamentals drive markets. This means possessing a macroeconomic appreciation of how changes in interest rates impact the economy, how foreign exchange rates influence monetary policy, or what impact government deficit spending will have on growth projections. Certain types of trading demand more knowledge of the markets than other kinds. A quant trader, for example, will not need as strong a background in economics as a person concentrating on fundamental macro, where such knowledge is absolutely critical.

Specific education requirements, of course, will vary between firms and will depend on which area of trading you are looking to enter. Strong proficiency in math, statistics,

Employers will probe candidates' general understanding of statistics and their ability to rapidly apply probability and calculate expected values. A favorite question, based on an 18th-century French betting game, poses the following to interviewees:

Let's play a game I just invented. The rules are simple. I flip a coin. If it comes up heads, you pay me a dollar and the game is over. If it comes up tails, I flip again. If it comes up heads the second time, you pay me two dollars, and the game is over. If it comes up tails again, I flip a third time. Heads, we double the amount, and you pay me four dollars, and the game is over. Tails, I flip again. And so on and so on, each occasion doubling the payout for heads, or flipping again for tails. How much would I have to pay you up front to play this game?[1]

To answer in mathematical terms, a problem that is similar in nature to the daily choices made by traders, an interviewee needs a solid understanding of probability and expected value, along with an intuitive feel for statistics and risk management. There's not necessarily a right answer to this question, but an interviewer can learn a lot about a candidate's risk tolerance and risk awareness from the way he or she answers the above question. A person playing the game, after all, is exposed to unlimited risk. While there's low probability that he or she will lose $1,000, the possibility does exist. Is the candidate even aware of this risk?

---

1   "Here's How to Answer Goldman Sachs' Interview Question Based on an 18th Century French Betting Game," February 19, 2014, http://www.businessinsider.com/goldman-sachs-martingale-analysis-2014-2.

computer programming, and economics, however, should set you up well for most entry-level trading jobs.

DEVELOPING YOUR PASSION

It may seem obvious, but being able to display a passion for the industry is a basic requirement in the hiring process.

This is an industry where you have to be "all-in." If you lack passion, then the constant on-the-job learning demands will feel onerous and boring. Those who survive the attrition are the ones with a passion so deep that they become true students of the craft.

In interviews, I am often amazed by candidates who cannot answer the simple question of why they want to become a trader. These are the same people who, when asked slightly more intricate questions—say for example, what happens to bond prices when interest rates rise—cannot provide an educated response. Somebody with a passion for bond trading should be able to answer that question at an interview! You can bet that other candidates with the same qualifications—schooling, GPA, class placement, and quant and computer skills—will know the answer.

CHARTING MY OWN PATH

There are no shortcuts around the basic requirements. After a hundred FOAD letters, it became apparent to me that on paper, I didn't have the skills to land a seat on Wall Street like my more qualified friends. My bachelor of arts in general studies—a mix of pre-med and economics—with a low-A grade point average from a second-tier university in Canada was not making me stand out. All

I could manage, mostly through luck, was a position at a regional Japanese bank in Toronto. After conducting a rigorous self-assessment, it became obvious that I had to build a plan to insert myself in the top 20 percent.

Mainly, this required charting the right educational course. I returned to school for an MBA, and I specialized in finance. I did my MBA at the same school where I'd earned my bachelor of arts, the University of Western Ontario. Although the undergraduate school was considered a middle of the pack Canadian institution, the business school was the top one in the country and its students were well recruited by Wall Street. Although having an MBA is not integral, it does provide a candidate with an additional edge. After completing the program, I was the same person, with the same level of intelligence as on the day before I started the MBA program, but to the recruiters, I was suddenly a better candidate. When I sent out applications for summer internships after completing my first semester, I didn't get FOAD letters in response. Instead, potential employers called, wanting to set up interviews.

I did not simply go through the motions of getting an MBA. The sudden attention I received had as much to do with my degree as with how I spent my time in business school. For example, I took the liberty of completing a thesis, which is noncompulsory and uncommon at the MBA level. Aiming to pursue a trading opportunity in fixed-income derivatives, I did my thesis on Managing Convexity in Fixed Income Barbell Portfolios. It was an obscure, highly specialized topic that only someone in the industry would fathom. In fact, the idea came from my friend and mentor who was working in the same part of the business where I wanted to end up.

Although my professor didn't recognize the need to investigate such an obscure topic, the thesis served two material purposes. First, it provided me with an excellent education in this specific area of interest. I knew at this point that I wanted to work in the fixed-income side of the business. I was certain the people I was competing against for an entry-level trading position didn't know nearly as much about the topic as I did. As it turns out, I discovered many years later that my thesis was remarkably basic to anyone working on a trading desk, and the people questioning me must have known it. Still, they didn't expect me to know as much as they did at that point; the interviewers were evaluating me relative to my peers.

Second, the thesis demonstrated to future recruiters the passion and dedication I had for fixed-income trading. Some of my peers who were interviewing for trading posts were still unconvinced that they wanted to trade. Several were simultaneously seeking investment banking spots, which have no similarities to trading whatsoever. It was difficult for these candidates to convince recruiters they possessed a passion for the industry.

I knew that attending an MBA program wasn't enough. At the beginning of the degree, I set the goal of finishing near the top of my class, a goal I ultimately achieved. In addition to the thesis and class ranking, I took the classes I knew firms would want to see on my résumé, like math-related finance courses, statistics, and economics.

UNDERSTANDING REAL-LIFE ECONOMICS

During my MBA, I also carved out time to study the markets at every available opportunity. *The Economist* replaced *Sports Illustrated*, and each morning started with *The Wall Street Journal*. I read every book on trading and the industry I could get my hands on, including *Liar's Poker*, *Market Wizards*, and *Reminiscences of a Stock Operator*. I made a commitment to understanding real-life economics, a definite requirement for making the top 20 percent.

Today, with the accessibility of Internet resources and other media, there is no excuse for a lack of preparation when it comes to acquiring basic market knowledge. Watch CNBC or Bloomberg, listen to the podcasts of great investors, get a hold of Warren Buffett's investment letters, watch TV interviews with top asset managers, consume the publicly available market updates from investment houses, and scan the latest research from the Social Science Research Network (SSRN).

By immersing yourself in the field, you'll become familiar with the lingo and general way professionals describe and speak about the market and industry. Even if you don't become an expert in any one field, this course of study will provide you with the building blocks for becoming a professional. Also, it will help you determine a specific area of focus if you haven't yet located one.

FIND A MENTOR

The period during which you're working to upgrade your skills and learn about the markets is also when you should be meeting the right people in the trading world—from peers and professors outside the industry to junior traders and principals within the business—with the objective of establishing a network of individuals with the same interests or goals. This will allow you to keep tabs on what is happening in the industry. Down the road, when it comes time to search for a job, this network may pay dividends. Finding a mentor can be especially valuable at this stage, and it doesn't need to be a guru with decades of experience.

In college, when I switched from medicine to economics—still unsure of what I wanted regarding a career—I became friends with a guy who knew exactly what he wanted to do with his life. He was determined to be a derivatives trader on Wall Street. Back then, I didn't quite know what that meant. What I did know, or believed, was that Wall Street was a shark tank and New York was VERY different from the small Canadian town where I grew up. I was fascinated by my friend's desire to leave Canada—something I'd never considered doing—and he thrust himself into the biggest and most dangerous pool of fish around.

While we all stayed out late at the bars, this friend somehow found time to methodically plot his path to achieve his goal. Eventually, that undergraduate honors economics student from a mediocre Canadian school got hired to work on the J.P. Morgan interest rate swaps desk.

Immediately, he took on the role of mentor. The stories he told seemed like fiction: the lifestyle, the trading floor atmosphere, the responsibility for large sums of money, and, of course, the first full-year bonus. I now knew what I wanted to do after I graduated.

I was lucky enough to find a mentor who was three to four years ahead of me, and his advice was invaluable.

Through the years, I've paid it forward by mentoring young people considering careers in trading. If I come across a research report I think is especially pertinent, I'll send it their way. More importantly, I give them an authentic taste of the knowledge, culture, and work ethic it takes to succeed. Without this guidance, they'd be left guessing what the industry is really like, maybe even thinking it resembles *The Wolf of Wall Street*.

NOW WHAT?

You might find yourself in the top 20 percent of candidates by taking the right courses, improving your quant skills, learning about the markets, networking effectively, and developing a passion for the industry, but to get a seat on a trading desk, you need to get through the interview process, which means having the right set of soft skills. Just as some people fail the interview because they cannot explain what happens to bond prices when interest rates go up, candidates get rejected because they don't have the right personality to work in team situations. Traders, after all, spend day after day sitting shoulder-to-shoulder with their colleagues. The ability to develop and finesse interpersonal skills can mean the difference between landing a role or being forced to find a new field.

CHAPTER THREE

PASSING THE FOXHOLE TEST

Soft skills. You either have them or you don't, some people will argue. Some potential employers may dismiss them outright as inconsequential. After all, doesn't a company just want smart people who will perform well? In most industries, though, soft skills are integral to first-rate work. This is particularly the case in the world of trading—if you're self-absorbed, unreliable, or simply a jerk, it will not only be incredibly hard to secure a spot, it will be difficult to keep one and advance.

If I interview ten applicants for one opening, and they seem relatively equal in terms of hard skills and likability, the decision for me comes down to what Goldman Sachs calls the "foxhole test." If I were trapped in a foxhole for twelve hours a day during a long, drawn-out battle, whom would I want crouched next to me?

Needing to survive, I'd first make certain the person had the basic skills of any good soldier, such as being a good shot, having a solid understanding of tactics, and possessing the ability to use communication technologies. Above all, I'd want someone I could trust, whom I knew would have my back until the last bullet was fired, somebody who could keep his or her cool, and who could make the best out of any situation.

Life on a trading floor is similar. When assessing a candidate, I need to know the candidate across from me is somebody I can count on when the shit hits the fan in the markets and tensions are riding high on the desk. I need to feel confident that the person has the judgment, integrity, tenacity, positivity, and problem-solving abilities to do whatever it takes to get the task done correctly without making costly mistakes.

Traders aren't only dealing with markets. They're interacting with their colleagues on the desk, bosses, trade counterparties, back office employees, investors, and industry peers. Human interaction is constant. This is why, once you've made it to the top 20 percent, it doesn't matter whether you're in the top or bottom half of the group. What matters is how your soft skills complement your hard skills. More often than not, when I hear about someone who was forced off a desk, I can point to a certain soft skill that he or she lacked.

Trying to get a good read on a candidate's personality isn't always easy, especially in a thirty-minute meeting. Still, several techniques have proven effective for me as an interviewer. I like to try to immediately gauge the integrity and judgment of a potential employee. As a result of being a twenty-year industry veteran, I know I have more market knowledge than any candidate starting out in the business. Therefore, I initiate the interview with straightforward questions that become incrementally more difficult. The purpose is twofold. First, I want to determine where the candidate's knowledge tops off, since I'm looking to quantify hard skills. Second, we will eventually arrive at a point where the candidate doesn't know the answer, and I'm looking to see how he or she responds. Generally, this will give me valuable insight into a person's soft skills and how he or she will behave on a trading desk. Candidates who try to feed me long-winded answers full of bull convey that they cannot be honest with themselves, let alone honest with their colleagues. A trader feeding his desk false numbers and shoddy answers is exposing everyone to huge risk.

On the other hand, if the candidate across the desk from me admits his or her ignorance, maybe requesting time to work on the solution, I know I've found somebody I can trust. The humility of knowing what you don't know and knowing when to ask for help is a key element of trading. Despite years in the business and more than half a lifetime studying finance and trading, I learn something new almost every day. There's plenty I don't know and numerous situations in which I have to ask others for help or insight. It's part of the business.

It all boils down to IQ versus EQ. Hard skills versus soft skills. The hard skills open the door, but the soft skills get you through it.

THE SOCIAL SKILLS CHECKLIST

The importance of soft skills is best illustrated by looking at the field of medicine. All doctors have attended medical school and undergone extensive training to get their license. In the end, what makes some doctors better than others is bedside manner, or what we call a person's soft skills. In fact, recent research suggests that a "positive doctor-patient relationship can have statistically significant effects on 'hard health outcomes.'"[1]

---

1   "Why Nice Doctors Are Better Doctors," April 20, 2015, http://health.usnews.com/health-news/
patient-advice/articles/2015/04/20/why-nice-doctors-are-better-doctors.

For me, it's immediately apparent when a doctor has a good or bad bedside manner. Did the doctor look me in the eye when she came into the room? Did the doctor treat me like I was just a number, or a patient she genuinely wanted to help? Could she effectively communicate a complicated issue, appreciating the fact that I have significantly less knowledge of medicine?

Like a doctor, a trader needs excellent interpersonal skills. Before going on your first interview, reflect on the state of your soft skills and determine whether they're sufficient to land you a spot on a trading desk.

POSITIVITY

A positive outlook may seem like an obvious requirement in any career. Such an attitude, however, is critical on a trading floor. Losses are common, an everyday occurrence, and it's easy for traders to feel as if they're constantly staring at a half-empty glass. A positive attitude won't necessarily prevent losses, but it does impact one's ability to rebound from them. Negative people have the potential to bring down a team, both in morale and performance.

When a trading desk is going through a rough spell, and there is a pessimist in its midst—venting about clients redeeming funds, the possibility of not getting paid at the end of the year, or employees being let go—the atmosphere turns toxic. Confidence is crucial for traders, and such negative emotions can rattle other members of the team and make them think twice the next time they need to execute a trade.

The optimist on the trading desk, on the other hand, constantly encourages his or her fellow traders to believe in their process, methodologies, strategies, and decisions. The optimist reassures others when markets are inflicting damage by highlighting the fundamentals of the trade that were right and explaining why the next attempt will work out better.

You cannot hide your attitude on the trading floor. You're not sitting in some corner office. Your teammates surround you at all hours of the day, and nobody is going to want to sit next to Chicken Little. Would you want to be in a foxhole with someone who always fears the worst?

LIKABILITY

Are you likable? Likability doesn't make a great trader, but it can be the difference between getting on the desk and staying, getting terminated quickly, or not getting an offer altogether.

If you have no clue how to be likable, a good place to start is Dale Carnegie's *How to Win Friends and Influence People*, which was first written in 1936. The traits of a likable person have not changed much over the years.

Carnegie's advice is straightforward:

1. Become genuinely interested in other people.
2. Smile.
3. Remember that a person's name is, to that person, the sweetest and most important sound in any language.
4. Be a good listener. Encourage others to talk about themselves.
5. Talk in terms of the other person's interest.
6. Make the other person feel important—and do it sincerely.[2]

Personally, I've always enjoyed working with people who are humorous, friendly, and positive. Above all, they must be genuine. If I like particular candidates, I'll want to help them—even if I don't end up extending an employment offer. If I really like them, I'll volunteer to mentor them once they are hired.

---

2   *Wikipedia*, s.v., "How to Win Friends and Influence People," last modified February 9, 2017, https://en.wikipedia.org/wiki/How_to_Win_Friends_and_Influence_People.

Creativity is an essential soft skill, since following the herd is not the way to beat the market. The best trading ideas are often the least obvious ones. Most investors limit their thinking and reaction to first-order market effects. For example, everyone believes interest rates are going up, so they trade based on the obvious consequences, like shorting bond futures. The savvy investor on the other hand will consider the secondary consequences or knock-on effects, of rising rates.

Howard Marks, the founder of Oaktree Capital Management, famous for his memos to Oaktree clients, describes the above phenomenon as "second-level thinking." In one of his memos, he writes,

"Since others may be smart, well-informed and highly computerized, you must find an edge they don't have. You must think of something they haven't thought of, see things they miss, or bring insight they don't possess. You have to react differently and behave differently. In short, being right may be a necessary condition for investment success, but it won't be sufficient. You must be more right than others... which by definition means your thinking has to be different...For your performance to diverge from the norm, your expectations—and thus your portfolio—have to diverge from the norm, and you have to be more right than the consensus. Different and better: That's a pretty good description of second-level thinking."[1]

---

1   Howard Marks, "Memo to: Oaktree Clients," September 9, 2015. https://www.oaktreecapital.com/docs/default-source/memos/2015-09-09-its-not-easy.pdf?sfvrsn=2.

Mentoring, as we discussed earlier, is critical in this industry. Mentors are not paid and they are under no obligation to help junior employees. They take time out of their busy days, because they have found someone they like, who they want to help and champion.

INTEGRITY

The conventional image of traders is that they play fast and loose with the rules. They lie. They use inside information. They manipulate markets. Yet integrity, which I like to define as doing the right thing when nobody is looking, is a key requirement of the position. If you lack this soft skill, it will only be a matter of time until you find yourself out of a job. Integrity, good judgment, and honesty are critical in an industry where each trader has the capacity to destroy the reputation, or even the existence, of his or her firm.

My integrity was tested early on in my hedge fund career. One day, as part of a complicated, multi-leg bond trade, I was tasked with executing a relatively simple transaction known as a "futures roll." We had a position in September Treasury bond futures and needed to switch the position to the December futures contract. It wasn't as easy as buying one and selling the other. They needed to be done in separate quantities, with the precise amounts depending on some not-so-straightforward calculations. I made my calculations, determined the appropriate ratio, and executed the trades.

Fifteen minutes after entering the trades into the risk system and getting some unusual numbers in return, it occurred to me that something was deeply incorrect. I double-checked my work, and the mistake was soon obvious. I had bought too many December contracts. But in that brief period, the market dropped, and we had lost $120,000. Completely my fault. Mistakes such as this rarely go in one's favor, and this was a hefty one, especially for a rookie.

Admittedly, at that moment of realization, my initial thought was to sit on my hands, pray that the market would bounce back in my favor, recoup the $120,000, and switch back to the proper ratio without anyone knowing. Fortunately, I had enough sense and integrity to immediately quash this thought. Instead, I marched right up to the CIO, detailed the mistake, and presented all of the available options for a remedy, none of which were very good. He thought about it for a hard second before telling me to sell the extra contracts and take the hit. After locking in the loss, I sat back in my chair, heart thumping, and waited for the ramifications, which I was sure would mean a pink slip.

The CIO's walk toward my desk felt like an eternity. Here it comes, I thought. I'm going to get terminated in front of the entire floor. Instead, he sat on the desk's edge and stared down at me. He put a hand on my shoulder and said, "You understand the mistake you made, right?"

"Yes," I replied.

"Okay, then. Don't make that mistake again."

Relieved, I apologized once more for the costly error. "I assumed you were going to march me right out of the office," I told him.

"You thought I was going to fire you?" the CIO chuckled with a smirk on his face. "Are you crazy? I just spent $120,000 training you!" He gave me a not-so-light pat on the back and walked away.

I never made that error again.

This could be a story about the importance of double-checking your work. We'll get to that later. The real message, however, is about integrity. If you trade for a living, you will inevitably make careless mistakes like the one I made. To survive the error, you need to resolve it with integrity, or you'll end up having to deal with not just a monetary loss, but also the loss of your career.

Mistakes happen. There are fat-finger episodes when a trader accidentally types five million instead of five thousand in the share quantity field of the electronic trading platform. A trade is entered into the risk system as a sell instead of a buy and the appropriate protocols don't catch it. Some traders hear that tiny voice in their head telling them to avoid owning up to the mistake and in the process, they turn a small problem into a much larger one.

Nick Leeson worked at Barings Bank in London in the 1990s. After suffering some losses from unauthorized, speculative trades, Leeson began using a special account to hide his losses. He was booking false trades and misrepresenting positions to management, and over a three-year period, the losses ballooned to $1.4 billion, or twice the bank's available trading capital. Not only did he end his career and spend four years in jail, but he also brought down a 200-year-old institution in the process.

RELIABILITY

A team is only as strong as its weakest link. Nowhere is this adage truer than on the trading desk. Traders follow a series of procedures, operations, and protocols before any trade is executed. If someone on the team drops the ball along the way, a routine trade can turn into a costly failure. Consider the examples of fat-fingers, or my miscalculated hedge ratio. Reliability on the trading desk means everyone has confidence in each other to get specific tasks done without mistakes.

"Glenn" was a key member of our back office, performing the critical work of correctly calculating the daily profit and loss in our portfolio of hundreds of trades. He was celebrated for his thoroughness and strong work ethic, but he longed for a position on the trading desk. In addition, he was likable and carried himself with a positive attitude, which is why senior members of the firm felt good about giving him a chance to prove himself as a trading assistant. Once he hit the desk, though, the quality of his work fell off considerably. Suddenly—maybe it was due to the pressure—he started to make mistakes that could have been prevented had he simply double-checked his work. He couldn't keep an accurate record of the real-time positions of the traders he was supporting. He became unreliable, and his errors slowed down and jeopardized the entire desk. Other team members no longer had confidence in Glenn's work, so they had to break from what they were doing to check and correct his calculations. It added another step to an already arduous process. After several months, Glenn was asked to return to the back office. He had a shot, but blew it, because he wasn't dependable.

WORK ETHIC

Hedge funds are demanding. Traders are expected to live and breathe the job, staying on top of market developments and geopolitical events even when they are out of the office. Depending on the markets you trade, this could mean waking up at 3:30 a.m. to track the European open, or staying up until midnight to follow a press conference with the Japanese central bank. You always need to be prepared, which takes commitment. This is one career where the minimum is never enough.

When I started at Merrill Lynch, my first trading floor experience out of business school, I was part of a group within fixed income called Global Debt Finance. We weren't assigned to a specific trading desk. Rather, we were placed in a pool with other rookies, and each of us did four rotations of three months at different desks of our choosing. The world, so to speak, was our oyster. We could request to trade Australian government bonds in Sydney, foreign exchange in Tokyo, or exotic options in New York, to name a few of the available choices. The goal was to learn about diverse products, so we could discover what interested us and whether our personality and skills would be a suitable fit for a particular desk. Merrill saw this as a way of limiting future attrition. When the year was up, business units interested in a trainee would send an offer for a permanent position. In a certain sense, we were still fighting for a job during that first year.

When I showed up on the first day of my second rotation, I was surprised to learn that "Peter," a fellow trainee, would be joining me for the upcoming three-month period. A friend who had been with him on the first rotation had told me stories about Peter, none of them too flattering. He took long lunches, stayed out all night, and showed up late and hungover to work the next day. During our three months together, he did nothing to rehabilitate his reputation. He was undoubtedly brilliant. He had done exceptionally well at an Ivy League school, and his hard skills exceeded mine, but he acted as if the trading desk was auditioning for him, and not the other way around. Whenever he asked me to cut out early to get drinks, I would ask incredulously if he had work, since I had it up to the gills. "I can deal with it tomorrow," was how he'd always answer. No surprise that at the end of the program he wasn't offered a chair at a desk and was eventually forced to leave the industry.

A trader needs to work hard, yet not allow the intensity of the effort to turn him or her into an unlikable person. For most people in the business, their careers are their number one priority. Not making the same commitment to your work will cause you to stand out in a negative way. Don't be the one who walks off the trading floor and heads home the minute the market closes. Your peers and your boss will notice.

The trading floor is a high-pressure environment. The constant demand of having to make quick decisions and generate profits creates perpetual stress. Each trader copes with these pressures in his or her own way. Some people deal with their stress by cursing at their monitors, others by going out for a drink at the end of the day.

When I was working at Merrill in New York, there was one bond trader who had a drawer full of telephone handsets. Every once in a while, when something was going horribly wrong, he'd slam and shatter a handset on the desk. The sound of disintegrating plastic was as loud as a gunshot. Without missing a beat, he'd reach into the drawer, pull out a new black handset, and attach it to the cord, as if it had never happened, other than having to pay for a new phone.

Whatever works for you is fine. Problems arise when traders become so enraged or stressed they cannot think straight, or their listlessness prevents them from absorbing new information. An inability to operate under stress is worse than having a socially unacceptable outlet for dealing with the pressure.

One morning, a month or two after starting at Merrill, the chief book runner at my desk left for a meeting. While

All sorts of shenanigans take place on a trading floor, and for some reason, many of them are centered on food. One of my friends at Merrill Lynch sat next to a man on the Eurobond desk named Ian. My friend had a sizable appetite back then, often buying two or three lunches. Ian was the opposite. He'd buy a sandwich from *Pret a Manger* that he rarely finished. One night they were out with the head of the desk and some other hitters from the trading floor, and drinks got rolling. Someone mentioned the Big Mac challenge: Finish ten Big Macs in one hour.

Ian put up his hand and said he'd take that bet with anyone. My buddy couldn't believe his ears and quickly raised his hand for $1,000, knowing how little Ian ate—call it inside information. In a matter of minutes, the bets approached $10,000. By the next morning, they exceeded $25,000.

Ian renegotiated the terms of the bet. Using his sharp negotiating skills, he managed to convince the group that if he could eat at least five Big Macs, he wouldn't have to pay out anything, making the bet a push.

Competition day arrived. Someone showed up at 11:00 a.m. with the ten Big Macs. At 11:30 the clock started. It was slow going at first. Ian took his time, giving his head every opportunity to realize his stomach was full. By 11:50 or so, he had finished only one and a half sandwiches. At 12:10 he had barely finished three, and he was starting to look a little green. Somehow, through extraordinary effort, Ian crammed the last two sandwiches down just as 12:30 came, with only seconds to spare.

One additional rule I forgot to mention: He couldn't vomit for 15 minutes after the last Big Mac went down, which he managed to accomplish before sprinting to the bathroom right as the clock hit 12:45.

The end of the trading day rolled around and there was still no sign of Ian. My friend was concerned, because he and Ian had dinner reservations with a bond broker at Gavroche, a swanky three-star Michelin restaurant.

My colleague visited the lavatory at around 4:15 and noticed a body on the floor in one of the stalls. It was Ian, passed out. My friend woke him up. Ian said he vomited for about 30 minutes straight until he finally collapsed from exhaustion. Rejuvenated from the nap, off they went to Gavroche for dinner.

Now is that stamina or complete ridiculousness? You decide.

praying that nobody would ask anything of me, a top sales-man came over to the desk and asked for a price to unwind a complicated basis swap. It was a time-sensitive trade for one of the firm's biggest clients, and I was still learning the details of how to value the particular instrument the client wanted to trade. Typically, the head trader would handle this matter while I watched, but I was occupying his seat that morning, so the responsibility fell on my shoulders.

My heart began thumping the moment my eyes locked on the work. Chest tightening, a dry sweat broke across my forehead, and I could literally feel my heart pound-ing. I was having an acute stress reaction, and it felt as if my entire body was shutting down. I couldn't remember formulas that were second nature to me. I couldn't even add five plus three. Essentially, I resorted to stalling tac-tics to buy time until the chief returned to the desk. He made small changes to the work I'd done. We didn't win the trade in the end. I was overly conservative with the pricing, which was fine because the last thing I wanted to do was quote the wrong level and lose money.

There are several lessons to learn from this episode. First, you'll never know the stress of working on a trading floor or how your body and mind will react in pressure situations, until you start trading. People brag about paper trading successfully, but the game changes when millions of dollars and your career are on the line.

One piece of advice I give to people looking to enter the industry is to begin trading your own account as early as possible. It doesn't matter what you trade. It could be stock indices, individual companies, bond futures, currencies, or soybeans. Whatever. Just start learning the craft in a practical rather than theoretical fashion. It's like training to be a pilot using a flight simulator before stepping into a real aircraft. It's not the real thing, but there's nothing better to replicate the emotions and decisions you'll face once you're in the hot seat.

The second lesson learned from my mini-panic attack was the need for a coping mechanism. At first, I experimented with meditation and yoga. Both alleviated stress, but neither could prevent its reoccurrence. Ultimately, the way I learned to manage my nerves was to constantly put myself in stressful situations and practice working through them. As I successfully navigated through the various scenarios, my confidence gradually increased, and the adverse stress reactions began to fade. It wasn't something I could learn from reading a book. Building up a tolerance to stress took years. Without this tolerance, I would have become part of the attrition.

Feeling stress or anxiety on the trading floor is normal. In fact, it's a worrying sign when a trader doesn't encounter such emotions. It may signal that the trader doesn't appreciate the implications of what he or she is doing.

EFFECTIVE COMMUNICATION

Unless you aspire to trade alone from home, you'll probably join a trading environment where colleagues are constantly discussing ideas and arguing viewpoints. Many of the topics are complicated and highly technical, and a trader needs to know how to articulate them in a comprehensible and efficient manner. If a desk needs to execute a trade, they cannot afford a thirty-minute discussion that should take only three minutes. Communication needs to be direct and to the point. In my own firm, we call this "Answer first." In discussions, we present the issue and the answer in the first two sentences of a conversation. If there is agreement, there is no need to elaborate. If people disagree, only then will we continue the debate. Learning how to articulate your point in as few words or sentences as possible without leaving out relevant information is a real skill.

Being a good listener and hearing the other person's counterarguments and ideas, is the other side of effective communication. You can't add value to a conversation if you aren't paying close attention to what has already been said.

Good salespeople are known to be effective communicators, and some of the best traders I've encountered could easily slip into a sales role themselves. Many hedge fund investors demand to speak directly with the risk-takers. They want to hear strategy descriptions in explicit detail— how the trader identified the opportunity, how they sized the trade, and what evidence could emerge to force them to rethink their position. Investors want to feel confident their money is in capable, honest hands. The trader, therefore, is tasked with helping foster a relationship of trust, and this cannot be accomplished if he or she is speaking past the client, constantly lapsing into technical jargon. Traders, after all, speak a unique language, using shorthand, acronyms, and a rushed cadence. The ability to express complicated concepts and ideas to someone with a fraction of your industry knowledge will make you the person clients want to speak with and a valuable member of the firm.

Effective communication is also about synthesizing sizable amounts of information into a coherent and relevant message. For five years, I served as an advisor to the Federal Reserve Bank of New York on its Investor Advisory Committee on Financial Markets. Powerhouses in the industry sat on this committee: Alan Howard, Henry Kravis, Louis Bacon, Rick Rieder, David Tepper, and Mohamed El-Erian. They were all brilliant, yet they weren't all effective communicators. In group discussions, some rambled on about one particular issue, while others would jump from point to point at random. Following their logic was often difficult. Whenever Mohamed El-Erian opened his mouth, however, the room grew silent, everyone sitting up a little straighter, and listening as if an oracle were speaking.

Now, he wasn't necessarily the smartest in the room, or expressing ideas dissimilar to what others were sharing, but he was more effective at communicating complicated ideas. There was a narrative flow to his speech, an ability to briskly lay out the facts and arguments, offering and rebutting potential counterarguments, before concluding. He had a knack for making his off-the-cuff remarks sound like a polished speech. Look up some of his television appearances and you'll quickly understand why I hold him up as an emblem of superb communication.

YOU LACK THE SOFT SKILLS...NOW WHAT?

The ability to develop and finesse soft skills can mean the difference between landing a job or being forced to find a new field. If you lack the personality to make it as a trader, it's better to accept that there are other opportunities in finance that don't necessarily require the same set of soft skills. Your personality may be better suited to becoming an analyst, salesperson, or back office professional.

Alternatively, you can make a conscious effort to improve your EQ. While difficult, it's not impossible. Taking a Dale Carnegie course, joining Toastmasters, studying your own body language, and recording and watching yourself in a mock interview are just a few possible ways to improve some of your soft skills.

The other option is to pretend you possess these skills. Try your best to be likable. Pretend you're a team player. Suppress all negative thoughts that enter your mind. Will it work? Even if you make it past the interview, you'll have to keep up this act on the trading floor for years to come. For obvious reasons, this doesn't have the makings of a winning strategy.

Everyone who has made it into the top 20 percent has hard skills that are "good enough." The soft skills are what will set a candidate apart. If you're fortunate enough to possess both, you're now ready to go after the role that is right for you.

CHAPTER FOUR

LANDING THE FIRST POSITION

HOW KARATE LANDED ME A JOB

Ask people in the industry, and they'll usually have a captivating story to tell about the interview that got them their first job. (This is not a coincidence, for a reason I'll explain later.) I have a story of my own from more than twenty years ago, when I was trying to get my start on Wall Street. I was in business school at the time, sharpening the necessary hard skills to make it past the initial screening process and had managed to successfully secure several interviews with potential employers.

For the first round of interviews, the firms generally came to campus to meet with the fifteen or so people they'd selected out of the one to two hundred applications received. Merrill Lynch interviewed one person after the next, each meeting lasting no more than twenty minutes. From this group of twenty, three or four candidates were invited to a second round of interrogations at the regional office in Toronto, where an even smaller number would be selected to advance to a final round of meetings at their headquarters in New York.

The gentleman from Merrill who interviewed me that day on campus was an old-school trader with a bit of an attitude. When I stepped into the office, his feet were up on the desk. It was hard to tell if he really enjoyed being there or absolutely hated it. He pulled my résumé off a stack of papers and began reading through it, silently, as I waited in my seat.

Finally, he said, "So, you think you're some type of tough guy, do you?"

"Excuse me?" I answered.

"You fancy yourself a tough guy," he repeated. "Says here on the résumé you do Kenpo karate."

This was not a question I'd heard at an interview before, and I was clueless as to how I should respond.

"I've been training for many years. I've fought in tournaments and passed—"

"Ever had to use it?" he asked.

"It's come in handy once or twice."

"Oh, really?" he said. "Tell me about it."

All I'm thinking at this point is how terribly wrong the interview is going. We're not talking about my Excel skills, or thesis on Managing Convexity in Fixed Income Barbell Portfolios. Instead, we're about to relive a college fight story. I resolved to hurry through the story and quickly turned the conversation to a discussion of why I was a perfect fit for Merrill Lynch. Soon, however, I was going into every detail of how my girlfriend and I went out drinking with some friends to celebrate a birthday. Leaving the bar, we hailed a taxi, and right as we were about to get into the vehicle, a guy holding a pizza came up to us screaming that we had just stolen his cab. He turned aggressive almost immediately, pushing the corner of the box into my stomach. I kept my cool, at first, but then he began spewing nasty words at my girlfriend, at which point, I threw a left jab that put him on the ground. He hit the ground, and a police car pulled up seconds later.

My ticket onto Wall Street was sitting across the desk from me, and here I was bragging about getting drunk and into a late-night fight. Done sharing, I wanted to get on with the rest of the interview, but he wouldn't let it go. He proceeded to ask what happened when the police arrived. After wasting another three minutes explaining how the police had seen the whole thing and agreed that I'd acted in self-defense, we finally reached the end of story.

"Knocked out dude with left jab," the interviewer mumbled as he scribbled a note on my résumé.

He announced we only had a few minutes remaining and asked if there was anything else I wanted to tell him about myself. An overview of my skill set came out in a jumble as I tried cramming my entire background into those final minutes.

Exiting the office, I pledged to never again make the mistake of getting lured into an off-topic conversation. Maybe I'd even take the bit about karate off my résumé. Three days later, I received one of the three invitations for a second round of interviews at the regional office.

At the time, I couldn't understand how such a seemingly disastrous encounter could earn me a spot in the next round. Now, as someone who conducts the same type of interviews, the reason was obvious.

After spending a long day interrogating fifteen candidates, the man from Merrill was sitting in his hotel room trying to determine who would advance. He'd seen so many. They all had the same credentials and many of them appeared to be fine people. Reviewing the résumés, he struggled to put faces to the names. Finally, he remembered one of the candidates he had interviewed. It was the karate guy; he seemed like someone with a good personality. The way he stood up for his girlfriend was a sign of integrity and steadiness, the kind of person others on a trading desk would like and trust. No question he'd have their backs.

SHOTGUN VERSUS SNIPER

Possessing both the hard skills to land you in the 20 percent of candidates and the soft skills that will help you pass the foxhole test, you can now focus on researching potential trading opportunities. There are two approaches you can take—the shotgun or the sniper.

The shotgun approach is one where you apply to all types of firms—hedge fund, bank, pension fund—for any kind of role—execution trader or market maker—in any market—equities, bonds, foreign exchange. This strategy can be fruitful if a thorough self-assessment hasn't successfully guided you to a specific option. Understandably, not everyone appreciates the differences between these trading situations, so it can make sense to use the application process to learn about the various opportunities before you narrow your search.

The shotgun approach requires significant effort since you apply to dozens of companies simultaneously. Still, the investment can pay off if it helps you identify a previously overlooked option. It will also lead to more interviews, and the more you practice interviewing, the better you will become at it.

The shotgun strategy is risky, though, because it displays a lack of focus. During questioning, an interviewer will often enquire about other opportunities the candidate is pursuing. If you're interviewing for a market-making job on the interest rate derivatives desk at J.P. Morgan at the same time you're seeking a role as an equity execution trader at an insurance company, J.P. Morgan will come away with the impression that the derivatives opportunity isn't that meaningful to you. Rest assured that the people you're competing against for the role will be able to articulate to the interviewer why the derivatives position is the *only* position they want. Worse, interviewing concurrently for a trading assignment and an investment banking spot displays an even greater lack of focus.

Let's use dating as an example. Some people use the shotgun strategy to find the perfect match. They ask almost anybody out on a date, expecting that only a small percentage will likely say yes. But has this process increased the odds of finding the right fit for a long-term relationship? Probably not. They'd be better off narrowing their scope to pursuing only the type of person they were genuinely interested in. This would also prevent them from coming across as desperate.

This is why I prefer the sniper approach. The sniper search demands focus, which is hopefully something you've developed through a rigorous self-assessment. Start by making a list of where you want to target and the role you'd like to play at those places. Then, rank them in order of preference and begin your search with those firms at the top of the list.

The sniper approach was instrumental in giving me my first trading assignment at Merrill Lynch. Once I'd arrived, I observed that my new peers in the fixed-income department all possessed this laser focus. It was where they wanted to be. I don't recall anybody saying that they'd looked for a spot in an unrelated field.

The sniper approach requires aim, but how do you pick a target?

TRADING OPPORTUNITIES

Recognize there are many types of trading, each with different roles and responsibilities. The three main types of traders are execution, market makers, and proprietary.

Execution traders don't choose what to buy or sell. Rather, they stand by and wait for a senior risk-taker or portfolio manager to tell them what to buy or sell. Then, it's the responsibility of the execution trader to decide the how, when, and where of completing the transaction.

I know someone who used to work directly for Steve Cohen at SAC Capital, one of the best-known and most successful hedge fund operators. He described the position as ultra-intense. Steve Cohen would stare at his multiple computer monitors before suddenly barking out an order. It was the responsibility of my friend, the execution trader, to make sure the trade was done at the best level possible. This required numerous decisions, which changed depending on the size of the order, urgency, and the security being traded.

Was he better off using an electronic trading algorithm or calling a trading desk to get a single price immediately?

He had to decide which exchange to use, and if it should be completed as a block order or in smaller increments. It was essential for him to have an up-to-the-second opinion on liquidity and order flow in the market. Professional execution specialists need to understand subtleties and details of the market that most amateur traders never even consider. Trust me, there's a lot more to institutional execution than hitting a few keyboard strokes when placing a trade.

Market makers, usually found at banks and brokers, play an important role for other investment firms such as insurance companies, college endowments, and pension funds who don't have any market-making activity. They service these clients quoting where they'd be willing to buy and/or sell a specified security.

If a client asks to sell a particular bond holding, for example, the market maker is responsible for coming up with a price where the firm is comfortable taking the risk. Similar to an execution trader, a market maker needs to have a good read on liquidity and short-term flows in the market in which he or she trades. Depending on these factors—among others—the quoted value is adjusted to be either aggressive or unaggressive. If the price is unaggressive and not to the client's liking, then the client will transact at another bank or broker where the market maker sets a better level. If the trade is done with the market maker, focus switches to how to profit from the trade. That may mean trying to sell the bond to another client at a higher price right away, or it could mean temporarily holding on to the position and making another trade to offset, or hedge, the risk.

The primary task of the market maker is to win business while still managing to turn a profit. Market makers don't have the luxury of determining what they want to trade with clients. Clients determine what instruments they want to trade; market makers just control the price at which they're willing to assume the risk. A market maker who is always ultra-conservative won't last long because the firm can only give itself a chance to earn money if it wins business. On the other hand, if the market maker is consistently too aggressive and winning transactions at levels where they can't exit trades profitably, then he or she will fail to hit the budget targets, despite engaging in high trading volume.

In 1994, I began my trading career as a market maker, serving as a trading assistant on a swap desk in London. I was assigned to the Italian lira swap book. This was before Italy joined the European Monetary Union and the lira was converted to the euro, so there were still independent book-runners for each currency. Any Merrill client wanting to trade an Italian lira interest rate swap had to go through our desk.

On our desk, market makers supplemented profits generated through trading with clients by taking risk positions on behalf of the trading desk using Merrill's capital. Without having to trade with clients, we could take directional or relative value market positions. We didn't have to wait for a client to trade. This is what's called proprietary trading, or "prop" trading.

Prop traders have complete discretion over all trading decisions. They're not setting prices for clients or waiting for someone to bark out a trade order. The ball is entirely in their court when it comes to the positions they take (as long as it is done within pre-set risk parameters). They can stare at their monitors all day long, just watching the markets move, or they can complete hundreds of trades before lunch.

Because of this greater freedom of choice, prop traders must be highly independent, confident, creative, and have a healthy appetite for risk. This is where an accurate self-assessment will again prove beneficial. If you're not a creative-type but are highly organized and methodical, you may be better suited to the other styles of trading. Some people perform better when given a specific assignment to execute, and their talent lies in improving the efficiency of existing tasks. Others don't perform well when limited to an exclusive task, and instead, prosper when given the freedom to produce original ideas. This is one of the fundamental differences between prop trading and the other styles of trading.

Your ability to articulate the position you want, down to the minutest detail, will help you set yourself apart from the competition. This goes hand-in-hand with displaying a passion for the industry and a broad knowledge of the markets. Also, trading desks are generally looking to fill specific vacancies, so if they're looking for an execution trader, and you can tell the interviewer why you're a perfect fit, you'll have a leg up on a candidate who only says he wants to be in the business.

The reverse can happen, too. A firm says they're looking for a prop trader, and you say you're only interested in execution trading. Such an admission could cost you the job, but it's better for you—and the employer—to not end up in a role that doesn't interest you and isn't appropriate for your skill set.

HEDGE FUNDS ARE A TOUGH PLACE TO START

Breaking into the industry at a hedge fund is difficult. There aren't many available positions and a majority of firms will only hire traders with relevant experience. Unlike banks, most hedge funds don't have formal training programs. Our firm, for example, is a mid-sized hedge fund, and we hire two or three summer interns per year. Compare that to a place like Morgan Stanley that recruits close to five hundred college students per summer. Still, there are plenty of other types of firms that are looking for beginners and are wonderful locations to learn the business, hone your skills, and have a prosperous trading career. Regional banks, mutual fund managers, family offices, insurance companies, pension plans, and sovereign wealth funds are just some of the alternatives. These institutions approach trading and investing in distinct ways and can be great places to start learning about the markets.

Hedge funds are a tough place to get your start. Don't refuse to settle for anything less than a hedge fund position, or you may end up unemployed. Get into the industry wherever you can. Take any interview you can get, even if you're not excited about the organization. First, you can always say no if it's not a good fit, or a better offer comes along. Second, as mentioned earlier, going through the process will help develop your interviewing skills. Third, through exposing yourself to companies outside your purview you may end up learning something about yourself and your interests. Maybe you'll start talking to an asset management firm you previously were unaware of, hear about their trading methods and culture, and feel surprisingly at home.

When entering the hedge fund industry, the learning curve is steep, although it greatly depends on one's prior experience. All other things considered equal, a trader coming to a hedge fund from a Wall Street bank will likely have a shorter learning curve than someone coming from a pension fund or an insurance company.

The market making function of a bank provides a lot of responsibility to young traders, and along with that responsibility comes the burden to perform. It's a sink or swim mentality. I don't have the industry statistics, but I'm confident that bank dealers have the highest level of attrition in the industry. Many of these traders get too much responsibility too early in their development, and they end up leaving the trading world after a few years. On the other hand, it's great training if you can survive. It's akin to the training you get in the military: rugged, intense and unforgiving.

Conversely, hedge funds are more cautious than banks about immediately handing over risk-taking responsibility to someone with little experience. A gradual approach to trading authority is better in many respects. Most young traders cannot handle the pressure when they're prematurely put in a risk-taking role, and end up flaming out. Some are talented people who may have had more success had they been eased into the responsibility rather than thrust into it.

CULTURE MATTERS

Part of your hedge fund job search should take into consideration the distinctive work cultures present in the industry. In my experience, the culture of the firm where you work is probably the most decisive determinant of your happiness and success. An organization's culture reflects its values, core principles, and standards for how people interact.

No two hedge funds are identical in terms of culture, which is why it's essential to consider how a firm's ethos meshes with your personality. Ideally, the beliefs of the company should match your own. Unfortunately, it's difficult to fully appreciate the culture until you're immersed in it. You may not realize a bad match before it is too late, which is why some companies go to great lengths to avoid this situation.

Ray Dalio, the founder of Bridgewater, places such an importance on culture that he has written a book called

Principles, which explicates his management style as practiced in the firm. Quoting the Bridgewater website, "We require people to be extremely open, air disagreements, test each other's logic and view discovering mistakes and weaknesses as a good thing that leads to improvement and innovation."[1]

He believes this culture, which he refers to as "radical transparency," meets the requirement that all interaction is recorded, and cell phones are not allowed on the trading floor. This is critical to the company's long-term success.[2] The goals are to reduce unproductive politics and provide workers with honest, unadulterated feedback. He readily admits the environment isn't for everyone, but he's open and upfront about this fact, because he wants all potential employees to know they'll have to adapt and assimilate themselves into this unique culture. In other words, if you agree with the *Principles* philosophy, then Bridgewater may be the place for you, but don't expect the firm to accommodate its culture to your idiosyncrasies or preferences.

Every firm has a reputation, whether it's aware of this or not. In some instances, the management team carefully

---

1   Accessed September 25, 2016, http://www.bwater.com.

2   Alexandra Stevenson and Matthew Goldstein, "Bridgewater Manager Ray Dalio Defends His Firm's 'Radical Transparency,'" *New York Times*, September 13, 2016, accessed September 26, 2016, http://www.nytimes.com/2016/09/14/business/dealbook/bridgewater-manager-ray-dalio-defends-his-firms-radical-transparency.html?_r=0.

works towards establishing one. In other cases, external stakeholders dictate it. Mentors or other industry professionals are excellent resources to provide you with a general overview of a firm's culture and philosophy. Additionally, senior executives of many companies regularly speak at industry conferences and recordings of these appearances are easily accessible on the Internet. Culture is driven from the top of the organization. Watching and listening to the leader of a firm speak could provide valuable insights. Organizations are eager to distinguish themselves from the competition, and they readily promote their unique culture to both potential clients and employees.

SETTLING IS NOT THE END OF THE WORLD

Through research and self-assessment, you have the ability to locate an opportunity suited to your personality and interests with great specificity. Sometimes, however, the position you desire isn't available. It's better to settle for your second choice within the industry than take a position in some unrelated field. Slowly loosen your search criteria until you locate the best available option.

If there aren't any opportunities at the hedge funds that are at the top of your list, look at smaller firms not on the radar of most applicants. *Barron's*, for example, publishes an annual list of the top 100 best performing hedge funds. This is a good source where you can identify places that may be growing and looking for new talent. You might be surprised to learn that many of the best performing funds are not the largest ones. If that doesn't yield any results, consider looking at traditional asset management businesses that are actively managing money in the sector or industry you're targeting. In other words, keep moving down your list of preferences until you have some luck.

Many of the necessary personality traits and soft skills mentioned so far are essential for long-term success in the business. But you can't have a lasting career unless you get into the industry in the first place. It's okay to accept a less-than-ideal position. Within investment management companies, the back office—where the accounting is done and trades are cleared—is a great place to learn the business. From a safe distance inside the firm, you can observe traders at work, get a solid understanding of the mechanics of the operation, and gain product knowledge. Then, when you feel you have a solid grasp of the job, you can try to move to the front office. People do successfully transition from the back office to the trading floor.

On our credit desk, for example, we pulled one of the accountants from the back office when we needed someone with his particular skill set to sit with the traders and help monitor the P&L. He wasn't necessarily interested in a trading position and didn't have many of the hard skills we looked for at the time. He slowly grew out of the accounting role and started to help with the trading, managing to carve out a niche for himself. Even though he didn't possess the same quantitative capabilities as many of the new hires, he was extremely reliable and trustworthy. He has now been in the front office for twelve years.

My first industry experience was at Tokai Bank. It wasn't in New York, and I wasn't trading. I was processing loans in the credit department. For $18,000 (Canadian) a year, I input information into a computer and did an enormous amount of paperwork, which in traditional Japanese style had to be performed in a highly specific manner. In fact, one of my duties was to count the number of extra bankers' acceptance certificates we had lying around the office, and then recount them.

Fortunately, the bank had a small foreign exchange desk where it helped Canadian subsidiaries of Japanese companies convert Canadian Dollar profits back to Japanese Yen. I spent all my free time tucked away in a glass-walled corner office networking with a few traders. They took me under their wing and introduced me to charting, technical analysis, and the standard vocabulary used in the trading world. They also taught me the typical trading axioms, like, "Cut your losses short and let your winners run." The adage, "A missed opportunity is not a loss; it's capital preservation" was taped to one of the trader's monitors. I appreciated the tutorials, but I didn't fully grasp the significance of these sayings until I was working as a trader myself.

I desperately wanted to move away from my mundane loan processing job to work in the foreign exchange trading room, but at some point, it became apparent there was little room for mobility. Still, the experience at the bank helped advance my career. It gave me an introduction to trading, even if it was just as an observer. Without the bank, I may never have recognized the need for obtaining an MBA. Also, the relevant work experience would later demonstrate to potential employers that I was serious about finding a place in the industry.

LEARN TO REACH OUT

While traditional networking may not play as much of a role as it did in years past, it's still a critical step on your path to securing your first post. Traditional networking means attempting to get access to senior people in the industry and trying to get them to help you navigate or even bypass the existing hiring process.

While my experience at Tokai Bank didn't give me the start in trading I was looking for, it certainly provided insight into the Japanese work culture. I received an education in how to bow to your superiors, how to say yes when you really mean no, and how to make yourself look busy when you don't have a thing to do.

At the annual summer golf tournament, I was given another lesson. The first time I played in the event, I somehow got placed in a foursome with the bank's president, the executive vice president, and the head of credit. They were all members of senior management who had come over from Japan to run the regional Toronto office. Then there was me, who'd been at the bank for only nine months at that point. Even though there were only thirty people in our office, I don't think they had a clue who I was.

As we were warming up, I noticed there were three golf carts, each with a single bag strapped to the back. I waited for somebody to invite me to put my bag on their cart, but it didn't happen. Maybe they forgot, I thought.

We proceeded to the first tee. I watched as each of them hit their drives. The Tokai executives seemed like decent golfers, but nothing special. I'd be able to hold my own, I thought. Then it was my turn. The strangest thing happened as I stepped to the tee box. The other three members of my group walked away, got into their individual vehicles, and started up the cart path toward their balls before I had a chance to hit.

I quickly teed up and smashed my drive about thirty yards past the balls of the executives in the group. I picked up my tee and hurried after my ball, trying to catch up with the golf carts ahead of me. Did they even know I was part of their group, I wondered? They played their second shots and moved on towards the green, again leaving me behind to play on my own and walk while they rode in their carts. On the green, the three of them putted out and replaced the flag before I could take my shot.

This went on for the first six or seven holes until one of the Japanese fellows realized I was consistently bombing my drives thirty to fifty yards past them on every hole. I guess they were impressed, because at an average height of 5' 4", they weren't striking the ball very far.

After one of my longer drives, one of the men stopped his cart and shouted back at me, "Garth-san! You hit very long drive. You're a long ball hitter!"

They never did let me on a cart, but they did hoot and holler every time I crushed one down the middle of the fairway. The ice was broken, and they acknowledged my existence for the rest of the round. I was convinced I'd made a great impression with management, and I thought it was only a matter of time until I'd get a promotion and a chance to move into the trading room. Nope. No such luck. But they did refer to me as "long ball hitter" every time I passed one of them in the hallway.

Fortunately, because of the advancement of social networks and the Internet, cold calling no longer requires picking up a telephone.

Once you've identified your ideal position, there are many ways to build a network to help you locate opportunities and gain greater knowledge about your specialty and the industry-at-large. LinkedIn is one of the best tools you can use. A simple search will provide you with profiles of specialists in the area you are targeting, who you can then follow. Assuming these individuals keep their profiles updated, you should be able to get a good idea of the business model of their firms and view the media content available to the public.

LinkedIn is also a great resource to educate yourself on different industry and sub-industry niches. There are groups for quant trading, hedge funds, family offices, ETFs, and many others. By joining these groups, you can begin to appreciate the issues pertinent to players in a particular segment of the business. An appreciation of these topics will help you sound more like an insider when you start discussions with potential employers. Don't be afraid or embarrassed to contact industry professionals with questions. The worst that can happen is they'll ignore your messages. Others, however, may open a dialogue and become valuable sources of information.

Increasingly, the first place employers will turn when evaluating an employment candidate is online resources like LinkedIn. It's now imperative for job seekers to have a digital presence. Your online persona, your personal brand, is another way to distinguish yourself from your peers.

Several years ago, a high school senior who lived in my area approached me online. He was looking for an internship at our company before starting in an engineering program at college. In his query email, he had a link to his personal website, which he'd built himself. It took three minutes of surfing his site to determine he probably had the necessary hard skills. The website also demonstrated his seriousness about entering the business. This was a young man who was clearly in the top 20 percent of his peers. He came in for an interview, and after verifying his background, I offered him a summer internship.

BUILDING YOUR RÉSUMÉ

Over the course of my career, I've reviewed thousands of résumés. A solid résumé, in my mind, is about demonstrating that you have the basics and beyond. The person reading it should be able to identify the hard skills and basic requirements that put you in the top 20 percent, while getting a taste of the soft skills that will set you apart from the other candidates.

Your résumé should stand out, but in an appropriate way. Don't project uniqueness by designing a distinctive and elaborate format. Don't employ eye-catching, fancy fonts. If you're applying for an advertised position, review committees are usually assessing hundreds of résumés concurrently, and they know where to find what they're looking for. If they cannot locate the information they need, they'll assume it's missing, or just pass, because they're too annoyed. It's recommended, therefore, to work from a traditional résumé template. Thousands of excellent examples can be found on the Internet.

The content, though, doesn't need to be standard, and this is how you'll make yourself memorable and increase the likelihood of securing an interview. Consider sharing a relatable personal interest or accomplishment to build a connection with the reader. Make sure it's unique and true. Lots of people enjoy movies and cooking for pleasure. Listing such hobbies will not make the candidate memorable. What may catch the interest of a recruiter, though, is if someone were to note that he or she keeps a blog about spaghetti westerns, apprenticed under a Michelin star chef for a year, or rode on the college equestrian team. There is usually a group of people looking over the résumés, so you just need to successfully connect with one reader.

Brevity, clarity, and relevance are key to a successful résumé. Spelling, grammatical, and formatting errors are distracting and inexcusable, especially when applying for a job that depends on thoroughness and attention to detail. A new entrant into the industry shouldn't have a résumé longer than one page. The people reviewing the résumés don't have the inclination to read long essays; the key is to demonstrate how past experiences prove proficiency in both the hard and soft skills required for the particular position you desire.

The one page you'll use for your résumé is valuable real estate, and all material you put on it should be impressive and should relate to the post. Every piece of information should scream at the reader, "This is a top 20 percent candidate!" If 90 percent of applicants were members of their college finance club, then it's not a noteworthy achievement. But perhaps fewer than 5 percent were presidents of the club, meaning that's worth mentioning.

It goes without saying that your contact details should be up to date and provide a way for somebody to effortlessly connect with you. No candidate is so spectacular and indispensable that a company will waste its energy hunting you down.

Once, while looking for a summer intern, I pulled a résumé from a stack of about fifty. The candidate appeared to have the required skills and it was an impressive résumé. I was ready to call him with the good news when I discovered that his résumé was missing his contact information. He had forgotten to put his phone number or email address at the top—all I had was his name. I tossed it in the trash and kept looking through the stack.

Demonstrating soft skills, such as work ethic, integrity, reliability, and likability, on a résumé is difficult. How does an entrant, who has never worked as a trader, show an ability to take risks and deal with the accompanying stress?

Personally, I'm drawn to applicants who, through their résumé, can express a level of entrepreneurship. I'm excited, for example, to read about a business started out of a college dorm. This proves the candidate has an eye for opportunities and a willingness to take risks. If the business is related at all to finance, I'm even more impressed. The person may not have traded, but if he or she has any experience applicable to the asset management industry, this is better than having none at all. Again, it shows a certain level of commitment.

One the best examples of related work experience I've encountered was a student at the University of Oxford, which was a target school for the bank I used to work for in London. Part of my function was to help with the bank's college recruiting efforts. One day, a colleague and I boarded a train to Oxford to interview roughly fifteen candidates pre-selected by the human resources department. One of the students turned out to be a part-time horse racing bookie, which is how he made money to pay for school. He had to balance the flows of bets before each race and learn how to lay off his risk to avoid exposure to any event that could leave him with a large loss. This job as a bookie, which also demanded an understanding of odds-making and risk, was the perfect parallel to the work of a trader. My colleague and I identified him as someone we wanted to invite to the next round of interviews.

Even when you think your résumé is complete, make sure you have your peers and industry professionals review it before sending it out. You may even consider using a résumé-writing service to optimize your end product. Your résumé, in combination with your online personal brand, will hopefully land you in front of the right people who will help you break into the industry, assuming you get through the interview process.

INTERVIEWS: ONE CHANCE TO MAKE A GOOD IMPRESSION

It's difficult to undo a bad first impression. This is particularly the case when being interrogated by traders, who are conditioned to make quick decisions. They're in the business of looking for a reason to say no more than an excuse to say yes, and once they determine they're going down a route, it's hard for them to turn back. I've never decided to hire anyone within the first two minutes of an interview, but I've dismissed candidates because of limp handshakes, inappropriate dress, or because they didn't look me in the eye when we first met. Often, you can't put your finger on exactly what creates a first impression, whether good or bad. That's why it's called an "impression." It's an idea or feeling formed without conscious thought. All interviewers have their biases, and these tend to rule the day.

Nevertheless, nobody should need to tell you that showing up to the meeting unshaven, in a stained shirt untucked over a pair of shorts is inappropriate and disqualifying. Research the firm you're visiting and learn about its culture, so you don't show up to the interview under or overdressed—though it's better to err on the side of overdressed. Just don't wear a tuxedo; nobody likes a smart ass.

Let's start with some basics. A strong handshake is mandatory. A weak one, or an awkward one, leaves a negative impression. Having said that, one candidate, who was a 6′ 4″, 240-pound former college football player, absolutely crushed my hand. There's a difference between strong and painful!

Pay attention to your body language, which can either convey confidence or timidity. The latter is not the message you want to communicate during an interview. Strong posture is critical. Do not slouch, put your foot up on a chair or table, or nervously shake your leg. Sit up straight, your rear pressed against the back of the chair, and your head held up high. Keep those palms dry to the best of your ability. Smile, make eye contact, and respond enthusiastically when others speak to you. Try to build rapport immediately through some light, inoffensive conversation—even if it's about the weather or last night's ball game. (Amy Cuddy's TED talk on body language, which has over 40 million views, is well worth a watch.)

Your résumé will usually be in front of the interviewer. Sometimes he or she will want to walk through the résumé with you; other times, the interviewer will not even glance at it. Instead, they'll initiate a casual conversation. I'm in the latter camp. The candidate has been invited for an interview because we liked what we saw on the résumé, but now I want to hear and see how he or she speaks and communicates. Can the candidate explain why he or she chose a career in trading? Why did they target our shop? Could I see myself trapped in a foxhole with this person? I want to hear succinct, articulate, and sincere answers, which is how traders are expected to communicate once they hit the floor.

I may ask the interviewee to tell me what's happening in the market that day. After all, if markets are truly a passion, he or she would probably know, even without preparing for an interview. Moreover, I like to hear the depth of the candidate's views. This indicates whether the person engages in independent thought or simply regurgitates the herd mentality as written on the front page of *The Wall Street Journal.* On a trading desk, you need to be able to transmit relevant information in a clear, concise manner. Traders, especially senior ones, cannot afford to waste precious moments on clarifications or a hesitant analysis.

Tone is particularly important when communicating during an interview. In my opinion, injecting a little tasteful humor and lighthearted, unscripted banter is the best way to come across as confident and memorable. A good sense of humor is appreciated on a trading desk, since it helps alleviate the stress. This doesn't mean you should come into the interview armed with jokes, but keep your tone light, even when discussing serious matters like the market.

Truthfully, from the interviewer's perspective, most discussions are boring and tedious. Applicants tend to come in anxious or overly serious, making the interview an even less enjoyable experience for the person sitting across the desk. Speaking breezily, therefore, will allow you to stand out. It will reveal an authentic, confident, and likable personality.

Confidence is good, but there's a fine line between confidence and cockiness. Confidence is when someone knows he or she can complete a task. It's having the belief that raw skills will translate into high performance. Confidence is accompanied by humility, the openness to the possibility of error. If a confident trader doesn't know the answer to

Most think of Goldman Sachs as a highly secretive organization, but through various online forums and websites, one can easily find a list of the sorts of questions they typically ask during interviews. The bank is interested in discussing an applicant's CV in great detail. If a candidate claims he or she took a Python programming course back in college, the person should expect to discuss it in detail. They'll also work quickly to gauge your interest in the industry.

Here are some sample questions:

1. Which was your preferred class at university?

2. What motivates you in life?

3. Why Goldman Sachs?

4. What's more important—deadlines or the quality of work?

5. Tell me about yourself. You have three minutes.

6. Discuss a deal you have read about recently.

7. Which is the best method of valuing a company and why?[1]

---

[1] "Goldman Sachs Interview Questions, the Definitive List," October 28, 2016, http://news. efinancialcareers.com/uk-en/220502/goldman-sachs-interview-questions-the-definitive-list/.

a difficult question, he or she is not too proud to admit ignorance. They may not have the answer right then and there, but they know they are smart enough to do the work necessary to come up with the correct answer if given the latitude. I like people who are confident in their abilities.

Cockiness, on the other hand, is when people are confident about their knowledge. The cocky candidate comes into the interview thinking there's nothing left to learn.

He or she believes that admitting ignorance is a complete repudiation of him or her as a person. A risk-taker closed off to the possibilities, and even likelihood, of errors, mistakes, and losses, can produce disastrous results. Never be afraid to acknowledge ignorance during an interview. There's only so much you can be expected to prepare for.

Expect the unexpected. Some interviewers will lead with questions, while others will sit back and stay quiet, insisting the person across the table do the work of selling themselves. Others will subject the candidate to various trick questions, as we discussed earlier, like the popular coin-flipping proposition, or my personal test of seeing how interviewees respond to not knowing an answer.

In our firm, one senior member relishes testing the candidates' hard skills. If someone identifies him or herself as a person well versed in software code, this senior trader might walk into the interview, briefly introduce himself, hand the applicant a laptop, and request that the candidate solve a certain problem and write it up in code. If a candidate boasts of having received a 4.0 average in calculus, this senior member might furnish a math problem. The test enables him to verify the applicant's competence, and more importantly, whether the person can utilize his or her hard skills in a pressure situation. Beyond this, witnessing how a candidate approaches the test provides an additional glimpse into the person's soft skills. Does the applicant work quickly and efficiently under pressure? If so, does it come at the expense of thoroughness? And, of course, how does the person react to not knowing an answer?

Anything is possible when it comes to the format. There can be several interviewers or a group of people. At our shop, we've had situations in which seven people were surrounding one candidate. You may have a single interview that lasts twenty minutes or five separate ones lasting a total of six hours. When I flew to Florida from London to meet with the hedge fund where I work now, I was interviewed continuously for thirty-six hours and ended up sleeping over at one of the interviewer's houses.

The "good cop, bad cop" routine is a common tactic for employers as it allows them to see how the candidate responds to stress and adversity.

The format depends on where you are in the hiring process and who is conducting the interview. Prepare for potential hiring scenarios by keeping your nerve and staying confident in the abilities you possess. Be yourself and never get aggravated over the knowledge you lack.

Of course, interviews are going to be stressful, but your goal is to avoid making your anxiety painfully obvious.

Fortunately, interview skills can be developed, and practice is the only way to improve.

PLAY TO WIN

Imagine you are in a tiebreaker in the Wimbledon final. You can approach the tiebreaker in two distinct ways. You can come out super aggressive, targeting the lines on each shot, or you can play cautiously, hoping your opponent's nerves take over and cause him or her to start making unforced errors. In other words, you can either play to win or to not lose. There's a big difference. If you don't play to win, you're choosing defense over offense, hoping your opponent makes a mistake. This is not playing with confidence in your skills.

The natural tendency from the perspective of most candidates is to try to not screw up and say something stupid or disqualifying. There's a temptation to say what you believe the interviewer wants to hear. Playing it safe, however, is playing to lose. Once you get to the final stages, there is a level playing field. Everybody who is trying to get on the trading floor is smart. The competition boasts of comparable or superior hard skills, and the other people interviewing that day probably all look identical from the interviewer's point of view. Providing scripted, canned answers to questions won't help you distinguish yourself from the pack.

Playing to win means engaging in a conversation, not merely answering a question when asked. The interview shouldn't be a "yes" or "no" answer session. It's about making sure you get your key points across to the interviewer regardless of the direction of the discussion. At this stage, you must sell yourself.

Most interviews end with the interviewer asking if the candidate has any questions. This is your final chance to stand out and be memorable. Avoid asking anything you could learn from a simple Internet search. Enquire about the firm's culture. Ask the interviewer to describe it in detail.

Another example of a solid question is one that seeks guidance. For example, ask the person what suggestions and advice he or she has for someone starting out in the industry. First, the question is personal, immediately establishing a connection with the person on the other side of the desk. You're asking the interviewer to take an interest in you and your career. Also, you're valuing the opinion of the person and showing a healthy dose of humility. Second, people generally like discussing how they started in the business, believing their story is unique and proof of their singularity. Everyone likes to believe he or she is an embodiment of a rags-to-riches myth. You never know, the interviewer may even provide you with helpful insights to benefit your career.

EVERY INTERVIEW COUNTS

After receiving almost fifty FOAD letters—another fifty places didn't even bother responding—I finally got a positive response. I received a request for an interview. It was from the Japanese bank mentioned earlier. Luck played a major role, no question. My résumé happened to get in front of the right person at the right time. After so much rejection, I was convinced this would be my only shot and my one chance to break into the industry. At this point, there was no plan B.

The office was small, thirty workers at most, almost all of them Japanese. The first interview was with a woman from the human resources department, who was one of the few fluent English-speakers at the bank. The interview was quite standard: Tell us about yourself. What are your strengths and weaknesses? What was your favorite subject in school? She was looking for obvious red flags, probing to see whether I was a level-headed person who could work well with others.

The second meeting was with a manager in the credit department who spoke little English in a thick Japanese accent. "When you were in school..." were the only words I could make out from his first question. I told him I didn't understand and asked him to repeat the question. Again, all I managed to get were those first few words. I had no idea what he wanted from me. I asked him to repeat the question, once more, but it wasn't any clearer the third go-around. Unable to understand, I didn't know what to do. I could see he was growing uncomfortable. If I asked him to repeat the question again, it would effectively end the interview, since it would establish an inability to communicate, or, therefore, work together.

At that moment, I realized English was my strength and obviously his weakness. I decided to gamble. I leaned forward, smiled, and working off the five words of the question I understood, started to share all details that were possibly relevant from my undergraduate education. The courses I took, why I was qualified for the job, and so on. Immediately, he lifted his chin, squinted his eyes, and nodded along as I spoke uninterrupted for the next ten minutes. After I'd finished, we stood, shook hands and bowed. Two days later, the bank called to tell me how much the manager enjoyed our meeting and wanted to offer me a position. I accepted it on the spot, marking my first foray into finance.

Be prepared for anything. People often don't remember or even necessarily hear what you say. They remember how you say it. The situation didn't allow me to convey content, but I could express confidence, charisma, enthusiasm, and positive energy. This led to my first real insight into how to get hired. When face-to-face, soft skills can tell you more about a candidate than their résumé of hard skills. EQ trumps IQ.

STAYING IN AND STANDING OUT

CHAPTER FIVE

MAKING A POSITIVE FIRST IMPRESSION

At age thirteen, my parents sent me to a boarding school on Vancouver Island. It was an all-boys school for grades 8 to 12. Other than my brother, who was one grade ahead of me, I didn't know a single person at the school. As one of the youngest students, I quickly learned the importance of striking a balance between conforming to well-established norms and standing out from the crowd. An attempt to swing too much in either direction would land me in conflict with either the surrogate parents—the staff—or my peers. I had to learn when to stand up and when to stand down. I witnessed new students make social blunders in the first week of school that would haunt them for years.

The boarding school experience isn't for everyone. Living in close quarters 24/7 with so many people and their idiosyncrasies is bound to present challenges. If there's one valuable skill it forces you to learn, however, it's the ability to get along with others. That doesn't mean all your interactions are pleasant. It's more about learning to get through by getting along. There's simply no other option. You may have a super-cool roommate with whom you have much in common, or you could find yourself bunked with the biggest jerk in the world. Developing the ability to act cordially and respectfully towards my peers—those more senior than me early on and those younger than me as graduation approached—proved to be an asset when I initially found myself on a trading floor, another environment with close quarters.

First impressions are decisive when it comes to interviewing, as discussed in the last chapter. They're equally critical when you arrive at your new firm. The last thing you want to do is create a damaging reputation early on. This is sound advice regardless of whether your first assignment is on a trading floor or not. It will take a while to appreciate the firm's culture and norms. In the meantime, avoid rubbing your new co-workers the wrong way. Recognize that you're starting at the first rung on a tall ladder. Everybody in this business begins in a junior role. Come to peace with the fact that there will be a prolonged period—possibly years—and many trials until you are trusted to become a full-fledged trader. This is a time for patience.

Some new recruits have difficulty accepting this reality. Those fortunate enough to land trading desk opportunities are people who are generally accustomed to success. They've been selected from hundreds of other candidates and are considered the proverbial cream of the crop. At every station in life until now—school, sports, prior employment—they've had success, and they carry an expectation to immediately shine in any new situation. Lasting in this business, however, requires tempering any over-eager attitudes.

ASSIMILATION IS YOUR FIRST ORDER OF BUSINESS

The trading floors of most hedge funds are filled with people of varying backgrounds. Some went to Ivy League schools, but others may have attended lesser-known institutions. Some have PhDs in their disciplines, while others never pursued post-secondary degrees. Some traders on the floor have thirty years of industry experience, and others are brand new. What they have in common, however, are smarts, talent, and an intense drive to succeed.

Anyone fortunate enough to join a trading desk arrives as just another member of the team, although the one with the least experience. The firm realizes it isn't hiring a specialist who brings a certain trading expertise to the desk. They're hiring raw talent with potential. Not understanding the jargon or exactly what others are doing at the beginning is perfectly normal. This shouldn't cause you to feel deflated or discouraged. Trading floor terminology will be learned little by little along with the rest of the knowledge needed to become a competent trader.

You cannot train for this job; the job trains you. Similarly, at the outset, the benefit of the employer/employee relationship is largely lop-sided, with the benefit primarily accruing to the new employee. A substantial amount of training needs to occur before a new recruit can add value to the trading desk. There's an acknowledgement that interns or neophytes on the trading floor aren't expected to impact the desk's performance on day one. Accept that you'll not add substantial value in terms of profitability for the first six months, which isn't the same as saying you can't be a valuable or valued member.

Assimilating into the group and the organization's culture is a new member's first order of business. The culture and environment of firms can diverge radically from one another. Some floors employ hundreds of people, while other trading floors are small, intimate groups of ten. In some places, the team atmosphere is prominent with constant communication between traders. Yelling across the room is encouraged so the entire floor can hear what's going on. Other desks prefer a serene atmosphere, where people communicate via chat, even if they are ten feet away. Absorbing the mores, philosophy, and ways of your firm will be accomplished through observing, listening, and talking to your co-workers.

As a new recruit, you must quickly learn and incorporate the idiosyncratic features of the culture. Pay particular attention to the people in charge. One of our head portfolio managers, for example, has zero patience for any frivolous noise on the trading floor, like ringing cell phones, music, or loud personal conversations. He is intent on establishing a cerebral atmosphere.

On one occasion, a trader was nervously clicking the end of his pen. Seconds later, a pencil went flying across the floor and hit him square in the forehead. He, and almost everyone else looked up, and the portfolio manager stared straight into his eyes and said, "Your clicking is killing me. Cut it out." Over the years, I've seen him throw objects at hummers, whistlers, and knuckle crackers, too.

If nobody is using his or her cell phone on the desk, do not use your cell phone. If the traders don't leave their desks at noon to grab lunch, then stay seated and remember to pack a lunch the following day. Don't wear a golf shirt, if everybody else is in button downs, and don't grow stubble if all the men are clean-shaven. Some of these firm-specific norms are told to new employees in advance, but often they are not, leaving employees to figure it out for themselves.

FIND A GOOD MENTOR

Your early days aren't a time to stand out, but an opportunity to assimilate, so your fellow traders begin to think of you as another member of the team. Watching the behavior of your peers can help, but having a mentor to guide you is particularly useful. Look either to the person who hired you, or to one of the seasoned members of the desk who knows the culture and has experience grooming newbies. A good mentor is someone who, on day one, can put things into perspective for you and continue providing guidance as you move up the ranks and meet greater responsibilities.

Hopefully, your role in the firm will progressively evolve and you'll move from an assistant to trader and, finally, to portfolio manager. A long career involves scaling one ladder and finding yourself at the bottom rung of the next one. Each transition will require the acquisition of new skills and responsibilities. In many ways, the need to assimilate and learn never ends. A good mentor can help guide you through these progressions.

The most senior member of the firm isn't an ideal mentor, since he or she will probably not have a lot of time for you. You need to have your mentor's ear whenever a problem arises, so you can take the appropriate action, especially if it's an urgent matter. Also, it has probably been years since a senior member worked as an assistant and they might have difficulty relating to any questions or concerns. They may view whatever you're asking as irrelevant, a complaint, or a sign that you're having difficulty adjusting.

A fitting mentor, in my experience, is someone three-to-five years ahead of you in the process. This person has spent enough time in the organization to know the culture and how it operates, yet he or she is not far removed from your current station, meaning the mentor will be more sympathetic to your difficulties and worries. Your mentor could be your direct boss, but it will more likely be another trader on the desk.

Let me repeat what was stated earlier: Nobody is getting extra pay to mentor you. The person will want to take on this informal role because you're likable. The process of securing a mentor is similar to finding a friend. Generally, it's a meeting of minds and personalities. The person you find should be someone who wants to see you succeed, and who has already achieved the success you desire. Look at the person's career and standing in the office. Ask yourself if this is an exemplary role model. Does the person have the career you want? Does the person appear to have the respect of his or her peers?

YOU ARE THERE TO HELP

New recruits, understandably, want to make a difference the moment they land on a trading desk, but you should fight the temptation to carve out a name for yourself early on. Over your first few weeks, you'll be meeting traders and back office personnel for the first time. Impress upon them the notion that you're there to help, not to solve the desk's problems, or to become its future head. If you try to stand out too early, chances are you'll fall flat on your face. By trying to show off how much you know you'll probably expose how little you comprehend about the business. Again, nobody expects you to be an expert on day one, and chances are the knowledge you do have will be quite rudimentary. You're the equivalent of a white belt in martial arts.

Years ago, when I started jiu-jitsu, the first moves I learned were simple defenses to standard offensive attacks—arm bars, choke holds, and the like. I remember thinking that once I learned these defenses nobody could get me in an arm bar anymore. After all, I'd successfully practiced the moves against other white belts.

I didn't appreciate that the blue belts above me were aware of techniques that totally negated my defenses. They could use my predictable reactions as a set up for more advanced offensive moves; for every attack, there is a counterattack. It takes the average person over a decade to obtain a black belt and effectively learn the multiple variations of all the techniques. Practicing higher levels of jiu-jitsu is akin to a chess match, where practitioners are required to aggregate hundreds of pieces of accumulated knowledge and experience in order to outwit their opponents.

Trading is like jiu-jitsu. Knowing one technique or style doesn't make you a black belt. The more you know, the more you realize how much more there is to learn. It will take many years to fully grasp the subtleties of trading and appreciate the inter-relationships of markets. The best thing you can do as a white belt on a trading floor is to absorb the basics while accepting the many unknown layers of complexity.

"We were born with two ears and one mouth for a reason," goes the popular adage. In other words, we should listen more than we speak. Good advice for all facets of life, especially when initially entering an unfamiliar environment. Processing ideas and thoughts before speaking or acting leads to more thoughtful and educated decisions. It's better to digest as much information about the new organization as possible before you stick your neck out and try to impress people, and it's better to say nothing at all than to say something stupid. There will be plenty of opportunities in the future to demonstrate your capabilities.

LEARN THE MANDATE

One of the first things you should familiarize yourself with is the investment mandate of the firm and its risk parameters. This includes understanding the basic strategy of the fund or trading desk where you work. How does the hedge fund and your specific desk, make money? Long-only, market neutral, short bias, macro, long-short equity? You should already know this, of course, but you need to consider the strategy when you begin to assimilate. It will help put your learning in context. Otherwise, your observations, suggestions, and questions will not be consistent with the firm's stated goals. In fact, they will be counterproductive.

Equally important is your awareness of the firm's definition of risk. Some companies define risk as the volatility of daily performance, with higher volatility signaling a riskier portfolio than lower volatility. They use methodologies such as VAR, or value at risk, to report exposures to portfolio managers and investors. Other funds focus on position size and leverage as the key metrics. Every shop has its own way of measuring and controlling investment risk, and it's crucial you respect these parameters.

"Darren" was one of the best new recruits, or so we thought. He came to us via a headhunter when we were looking for an assistant trader to work in our recently launched credit business. He had advanced quant skills paired with a personality that, at the interview stage, easily passed the foxhole test. From the day he started on the trading floor, however, he failed to appreciate that our company, like most other hedge funds, operated according to a specific mandate.

The mandate describes how the fund—or funds—is supposed to invest. Most fund managers specialize in a specific area, and the investors in the fund expect the investments to be consistent with their expertise. Some firms specialize in taking large macro-economic positions. Other places look to exploit small discrepancies in the value between stocks.

We concentrate on non-directional relative-value trading. This means we don't take a view on whether the market will go up or down, or if credit spreads will move in one direction or another. Instead, we attempt to identify mispriced assets, both rich and cheap, irrespective of how the markets are behaving. We buy the cheap stuff and short what we perceive is expensive. Traders and analysts are expected to make relative value investments consistent with this theme. Assuming they adhere to this strategy, they have great leeway to suggest any sort of trade.

Despite our clear mandate, Darren spent the bulk of his day crafting trades that deviated from our relative value focus. This was during 2005–06 when there was a raging bull-market in credit, and a majority of funds were generating handsome returns by simply leveraging their long credit exposure. It's as if our firm was an apple orchard, and Darren wanted to grow oranges. Our investors had hired us to grow apples. They weren't looking to us to provide oranges. This was our mandate, and it was clear to everybody what investments we could and could not pursue.

In Darren's mind, however, oranges were the smarter business, so he could never shift his mindset and provide us with the ideas and assistance needed to grow apples. He couldn't integrate into our trading culture. He was constantly coming back to us with more ways to grow oranges. Whether he was right or not was irrelevant, since we weren't in the business of growing oranges.

Style drift is when an organization operates outside the scope of its existing, approved strategy. Investors spotting style drift will usually redeem their money from the fund. This meant we would never be in the business of growing oranges, unless we specifically got the approval from our investors to do so. Meanwhile, Darren would paper trade oranges and boast of his imaginary returns. His attitude caused problems on the desk. Whenever a trade was proposed, he would criticize the fund's directive for the umpteenth time, reminding anyone who would listen that oranges were a better way of making money.

Within a year, we parted ways with Darren. It wasn't a good fit from the beginning. Several months after his departure, the global financial crisis struck the credit markets with a vengeance. Many of the funds that were growing oranges—going long credit—blew up. Not a great time to be in the orange business. In the end, after a few more stops at other hedge funds, Darren opened his own shop and built a moderately successful career, the perfect solution for someone unable and unwilling to work according to a team's particular needs.

ADDING VALUE TO THE FIRM

Most recruits begin working as assistants. Their function isn't to make trading decisions. Rather, it's to make the head trader's life easier. On any given day, a head trader has hundreds of tasks and responsibilities to perform, from researching the markets and checking P&L to communicating with middle and back offices and executing trades.

Every trader has a particular style and process. You should carefully observe him or her with the goal of figuring out how to facilitate the work. Begin identifying useful market intelligence to pass along that may have been missed or overlooked. Try to find a task that is part of his or her daily routine and see if you can do it for them. It might be as simple as printing out the daily risk report, or fetching a cup of coffee. The more time you can free up for the senior risk-taker, the more valuable you'll be to the trading desk.

Also, ascertain when you should and shouldn't speak to the trader. Leave your boss alone when the market opens and closes, or when economic data is released, and never bother your boss when he or she is in the middle of executing a trade. That's not when to start asking questions or talk about your weekend. Observe the other assistants on the desk, if there are any, and see how they interact with the trader they support.

The job description for an assistant is simple: Practice extreme service in anticipating the head trader's needs and do everything possible to execute your tasks correctly.

In the old days, before email, third party research out-fits would fax key reports at around 8:00 every morning, before the market opened. Traders anticipated these reports, wanting to know, for example, the outlook from various strategists on the economic data to be released at 8:30. One of my first tasks as an assistant was to pull the research from the fax machine, make twelve copies, and distribute them to the traders. Someone asked me to do it once, and I didn't have to be asked the next day. I understood that it was now my responsibility. If at 8:05 the fax still hadn't arrived, it was my responsibility to call the research firm to find out the reason for the delay. Telling the traders at 8:25 that the fax hadn't come in yet wasn't going to cut it. It doesn't sound overly complicated, I know, but failure to successfully complete simple tasks will prevent you from getting opportunities for something more advanced. If you're charged with getting lunch for the team, be the best damn order taker ever. Success as an assistant requires a "no excuses" attitude.

A trader will spend a good portion of the day on the phone speaking with economists, strategists, other dealers, inves-tors, brokers, and the back office. Ask experienced traders if you can listen in on these conversations; most trading floor phone systems have the ability for multiple people to use one line. Hear how they talk, paying special attention to the lingo. If you don't understand something, make a note and try to decipher it on your own. You don't want to disrespect a trader's time on a confusing term whose meaning you can learn from a quick Internet search. If you still cannot figure it out, ask for clarification after the call or later in the day. Keep a notebook readily available to take notes on what you've learned and what topics you need to come back to for further study.

Look for opportunities to increase the productivity of the desk. The constant development of new trading software, real-time data feeds, and visual analytics should be making the lives of traders easier, but some people are stuck in the past, using the same processes or technologies they were using five or ten years ago. The software or spreadsheets currently in use may be satisfactory, but there are probably many areas where they could be improved by being redesigned in a more contemporary programming language. Attempt to create an up-to-date, modern, and efficient system to save the trader—and yourself—time that can be spent on more productive tasks like researching new trades for the portfolio.

If part of your role as an assistant is to enter data into a spreadsheet manually, think of ways you can write an Excel macro to automate the work. Instead of the task taking half an hour, it can now take seconds, giving you valuable additional time to take on incremental responsibility. Similarly, if you're asked to create certain analytics of various market relationships on a daily basis, think about designing a database and a program to produce the analytics automatically.

Seeking out additional responsibility will help develop your skills. If you see a trader building a particular financial model, try to teach yourself how to replicate the work. Ask the trader to check your model and discuss some of the difficulties you may have encountered. It's one thing to understand a model and its inputs conceptually, but creating one from scratch requires a much greater comprehension of the details involved, details you will need to know to become an effective risk-taker yourself.

DON'T MAKE MISTAKES

We've talked about not wasting a trader's time with issues you can solve on your own. This doesn't mean you should never ask questions if an instruction or task is unclear. If someone gives you a project to complete, ask your questions at the outset. Don't spend a week working on it without a full grasp of the assignment. Don't hesitate to periodically check in with the trader to confirm you're on the right track.

The worst thing you can do on the desk is make simple mistakes. Mistakes, even small ones, display a lack of attention to detail and have an annoying tendency to cause trading losses. The markets are tough enough without unforced errors costing the trader, desk, and investors money.

There are many types of mistakes new assistants can make, but, at the end of the day, it's the traders who are responsible for them. If you provide incorrect information that's used to make a decision, any loss goes into the trader's books, and he or she is the one who will come back to you demanding an answer.

I've had assistants spend hours working on complicated spreadsheets and within fifteen seconds of looking at their work, I can tell there's an error. If the assistant had performed a simple sanity check, he or she would have identified the mistake, too. Obviously, sanity checks are easier for people to do once they have significant industry experience. It's much harder for a trainee to spot an anomaly if there's no understanding of what is normal. Conceptual errors are tolerated, sloppiness is not. Double-check, even triple-check your work before passing it along.

In trading, data is king. Part of the function of an assistant is to verify that the data used in the analytics is accurate. There's a saying in financial modeling: "Garbage in, garbage out." If the inputs into a model aren't accurate, the output will be flawed. Not catching incorrect data can lead to bad decisions, and bad decisions usually result in losses. When performing analysis, don't assume everything coming from databases is correct. Take a couple of minutes to scan the raw data and see if there are any outliers. If so, investigate and examine whether they are correct.

Say you're trying to locate a five-day moving average of a stock that is currently trading at 100. The values you've identified from your source for the previous days are as follows: 100, 102, 99, 201, and 101. Clearly, an assistant would need to examine whether the one-day price of 201 is a possible error. This one number, when fed through different analytics, may mean the difference between a trader choosing to sell a security or buying more. First, try to substantiate data on your own. If you cannot verify the data point, take it to the head trader for a second opinion before using it in your calculations. The above example is an obvious case. Still, it illustrates the necessity of avoiding errors and emphasizes the "no excuses" philosophy.

As a rule of thumb, the blunders that lead to trading losses are the worst ones to commit. Forgetting to put extra cream in somebody's coffee is different from inputting a trade backwards in the risk system. When mistakes happen, and they will happen, you need to be honest and upfront with yourself and others in the office. Integrity is crucial. Owning up to your errors is the only option, because traders can smell an excuse a mile away. You can't afford to lose the respect of your peers through dishonesty. Mistakes are easier to clean up the sooner you admit to them.

BONUS TIME SHENANIGANS

The distribution of bonuses at a Wall Street bank or hedge fund should be a joyful period. Everybody is hoping to get rewarded handsomely for his or her hard work the previous year. This is especially true for trading assistants, who, in lieu of a direct payout from trading profits, are usually paid in salary and bonus. The bonus can be a multiple of one's base salary, which is why there's a lot of angst surrounding "the number." For the employer, it should be equally thrilling to see an employee's eyes light up as that employee is handed a check for more money than they've probably ever seen. Bonus time is an opportunity for employers to express how much they appreciate employees, and for the workers to feel fortunate to have a seat on the floor.

Sadly, it never turns out this way. Bonus discussions end up being the most uncomfortable and unpleasant moment of the year for nearly everyone in the financial industry.

Bonus size is the scorecard. It's how people grade their performance. For trading assistants, the bonus is usually set in a tight, predetermined range. For more experienced traders, there is no such range. Traders immediately evaluate their number relative to their expectations. Is the bonus growing? If so, at what pace? Quickly, he or she will work out whether the amount is considered excellent, fair, or poor, and whether there is an embedded message from the bosses. Most people go into the compensation meeting anchoring their expectations to a particular number. These are individuals with type-A, aggressive personalities who live for competition, and bonuses provide them with one more area where they can compete with colleagues and themselves. Unfortunately, these personality traits often lead to an inflated sense of monetary self-worth. "I wish I could buy you for what you're worth, and sell you for what you think you are worth," a saying in the industry goes. This is why nine times out of ten, disappointment rules the day.

When assessing their bonuses, some traders fail to appreciate the many factors that go into determining the number. They tally their personal accomplishments, but ignore the firm and desk's performance as a whole. They take credit for 100 percent of what went right and a much smaller percentage of the blame for what went wrong. Frequently, they make erroneous assumptions about the size of the bonus pool, failing to take into account the true numbers after all expenses are tallied. I've even seen people seek rewards for the trades they *didn't* do!

As previously mentioned, compensation costs are the largest expense for a Wall Street trading operation. To avoid continually escalating expenses, managers will often try to come up with a number sufficient in size to prevent someone from resigning, and no more. The company will rarely surprise a trader with a larger-than-expected bonus. Only if the bank believes you have a higher paying alternative at a competitor will they be more willing to meet your expectations. There's a game being played, and the employee's role is to never appear satisfied, to keep the threat alive that he or she may quit if the bonus is not adjusted higher, or if he or she doesn't receive a financial guarantee for the following year. The employer's role is to convince the employee that the bonus is more than generous and justified.

This is the Wall Street culture I came from, so when I received my first bonus at a hedge fund, I proceeded to feign disappointment with the number, even though from an objective standpoint it was fair and expected. One mentor immediately told me to knock it off, remarking, astutely, that I was acting disingenuously. I was still a little sore when a second mentor gave me the following advice: "You have to look at the big picture. Sometimes you'll get less than expected, and sometimes you might get more. If you continue adding value and making money for the firm, I promise you that, in the end, you'll receive your fair share. You may not get it every year, but over the long haul, the money finds its way to the people who are creating it."

Coming from someone who'd been through bonus cycles on both the distributing and receiving ends, his words were prescient. Eventually, I'd see the wisdom and truth of his advice. The handing out of bonuses is an occasion for joy and gratefulness, not a period to feel overly stressed.

Rather than use the year-end discussion to advance your personal agenda, it's better to use the event to show appreciation for the opportunity to be part of the team and seek feedback on where you can improve going forward. Being gracious never goes out of style.

Now, when I hand out bonuses, I usually try to frame the discussion. I review the state of the business and the performance of the trader's desk. I try to explain how the size of the pool is determined. Still, I can often see that the person sitting on the other side of the desk isn't processing any of the conversation. He or she is too anxious to learn the number. For me, this is a sign of immaturity,

Every now and then, employers make a mistake and get the bonus number wrong. The best course of action if you truly feel your boss has made a mistake, is to deploy the "24-Hour Rule." The 24-Hour Rule means you give yourself one full day to cool off and assess the situation. Angry, you may say something that you'll later come to regret. Don't complain on the spot to either your boss or your colleagues. Take the day to formulate a logical argument. Go to sleep, and the next morning you can decide whether escalating the issue is worth any possible negative consequences.

a failure to see the big picture. It signals to me that this person is solely invested in him or herself and cares little for the team or the business as a whole, an attitude that can have negative ramifications when the person is in line for a promotion.

STAND OUT BY STANDING UP

Volunteering outside your comfort zone isn't something you should do on day one, but it's a step you'll eventually need to take to move up the ladder. After you've been at the firm for a while and feel comfortable with the existing responsibilities, look to take on tasks beyond your current workload.

This is how I got my first big break.

Three years into my trading career, I was working in London in the fixed-income derivatives division at UBS.

I'd recently moved from Merrill Lynch with several other members of the derivatives team after my boss was lured from Merrill Lynch to grow the derivatives unit at UBS. At 8:00 one Monday morning, the head of the UBS derivatives group, my boss's boss, tapped me on the shoulder. This wasn't long after I'd graduated from assistant to trader, and I was trying to stand out among the other members on the team.

"Garth, I need you to do me a favor," he said, although it came out sounding more like an order.

"Sure," I responded.

"I need you to go to Hong Kong," he continued.

"Hong Kong?" I replied. I had never been to Hong Kong. "What for?"

He told me I'd find out when I landed. He seemed stressed and in a hurry.

"When do you want me to go?" I asked, as he was walking away. "Today?" I said sarcastically.

He stopped, turned around, looked at me and said, "Yes. Call me when you land."

Hours later, I was on a plane bound for Asia.

The London office had been getting P&L reports showing mounting losses from Hong Kong in the millions of dollars. The global risk report, which management relied upon to keep track of risks in the various regions around the world didn't show any positions or exposures that could generate such losses. I was being sent to investigate the cause of the bleeding and report back to the home office in London.

It soon became evident that we were dealing with a rogue trader situation. The primary risk-taker on the Hong Kong interest rate swap desk had accumulated massive yield curve exposures not identifiable in the daily report. The size of these positions was far greater than what would've been tolerated by the risk department. This was back in 1997, and the Asian currency crisis was just beginning to bubble, disrupting the interest rate and credit markets. The Hong Kong Monetary Authority quickly raised short-term interest rates from around 4 percent to over 20 percent to ward off currency speculators, completely dislocating the bond and swap markets in the process. The trader was on the wrong side of the market and the lack of liquidity resulting from the crisis had rendered markets untradeable. Figuring out how to unwind the exposure and stop the bleeding became my responsibility the moment I identified the problem.

Talk about outside my comfort zone! I'd never been to Hong Kong, knew little about the market, and didn't know anyone in the office. Fortunately, the majority of the desk spoke English, so I was able to communicate with the team. The assignment was extremely stressful, and I was required to report in daily to the bank's senior management. Despite only packing for a few days, the unwind took almost six months to complete. I lived in the Mandarin Oriental Hotel for the entire time I was in Hong Kong. The experience, however, was career changing. It ended up establishing my credibility and redefining my role in the company. Through that experience, I became known as a "cleaner," someone who could parachute in and deal with a crisis. There are always fires to extinguish, and getting the label as a problem solver is a fantastic way to advance your career.

GET YOURSELF PROMOTED

An assistant trader typically puts in three to five years before getting the chance to become a full-time risk-taker. The responsibilities during this period should change and increase significantly from year to year. Hopefully, little by little, you'll gain respect on the trading floor and get closer and closer to shedding the "assistant" moniker in your title. If you're not gaining more responsibility, then you aren't progressing.

I was fortunate to find a fantastic mentor early in my career. He took me under his wing and gave me lots of unique opportunities. He traded interest rate swaps, US government bonds, and mortgages, and I was his assistant. Since he wasn't day trading, a vast majority of his positions would stay on the books for weeks or months. He'd maintain his positions whenever he was out of the office, instructing me to keep him updated. Unfortunately, he would often end up in a time zone where reaching him during market hours meant calling him in the middle of the night.

I knew his positions like the back of my hand. Part of my duty as an assistant, after all, was to understand his thought process, and why he included those positions in his "book," or portfolio of trades. Occasionally, when he was away, market events would require certain immediate actions pertaining to the portfolio. When this happened, my first responsibility was to contact him, summarize what had occurred, and let him decide what action to take. In most cases, however, he couldn't be immediately reached given the time zone differential. If action couldn't be postponed any longer, I had no choice but to decide myself. After all, as you now know, making no decision in light of market-moving information is making a decision in itself. Once in a while, this meant minor tweaks, and in other situations, it meant adding or reducing risk to his portfolio.

Acting unilaterally without his consent was bold. When I'd finally get in touch with him and explain the situation and circumstances, he'd often get angry. Again, I'd explain how I tried and failed to contact him. As the person responsible for acting as his eyes and ears, I did what I felt was necessary to protect him and his positions. Sometimes my mentor would end up agreeing with my decisions, telling me I'd acted prudently. Other times, he would scold me for making what he considered the wrong move.

Although most assistants would dread the thought of their boss going away, I began looking forward to his absence, secretly hoping that all hell would break loose in the markets. I cherished the opportunity to show him I could manage the risk in his absence.

Meanwhile, unintentionally, I'd successfully moved myself into a risk role. I'm not recommending you turn rogue and start trading your boss's book. My situation was unique. What you do need to do is take the bull by the horns, especially when it comes to showing the head trader that you're ready to start taking risk. In the end, it's about knowing which boundaries to respect, and the ones you should leap over. There are cases when it's better to ask for forgiveness than to ask for permission.

Too much responsibility too early can backfire, which is why it's better to be patient than restless. You don't want to establish yourself as a bad decision maker, and your judgment will improve with increased experience. Trading is a craft that takes years to hone. Emotions and behavioral biases—kinds that don't appear when you're just paper trading—come into play when you're trading with real money. Make sure you can handle the risk before you ask for, or take, greater responsibility.

There's no magical day or event when you can expect to graduate from being an assistant to a senior trader. There are no set circumstances or standardized processes. A lot of it comes down to seizing opportunities to show you're prepared and making sure you execute without error.

One way to get risk-taking authority is to become the resident expert on a new product or market. Hedge funds are always looking to novel products or markets as ways to make money with existing strategies. Take the lead on investigating these initiatives. This usually means doing the initial groundwork to see if there's indeed a lucrative opportunity. It may result in the head trader appointing you to run with the product.

Battlefield promotions are another transitional path. Assistants need to be prepared for the possibility of their situation changing in a flash. We've discussed the massive attrition rates and high turnover in the industry. When a trader leaves a firm, the opportunity to fill that person's seat often goes to the next in line, which is, generally, his or her assistant. The assistant cannot immediately step into the role if he or she doesn't know the market with the same depth as the former boss. Battlefield promotions are usually temporary, but if you perform well and demonstrate you're ready, you increase your chances of keeping the position.

The role of an assistant trader is similar to that of a second-string quarterback in football. The backup quarterbacks on a football team go to all the practices. They're expected to know the ins and outs of the playbook. If something happens to the starter, they need to be ready to enter the game at a moment's notice and execute the game plan.

Tom Brady is now known as one of the greatest quarterbacks ever to play the game, but he broke into the league as a low-rated prospect. He was drafted in the sixth round—the one hundred and ninety-ninth pick overall—and began his rookie season as the fourth-string quarterback. Even though he wasn't starting, he still had to prepare each week as if he were. By the end of the season, he became the backup QB. The next season, in the team's second game, Brady took over for Drew Bledsoe, the team's starter, after a vicious hit from Jets linebacker Mo Lewis. He would never relinquish the post, becoming the youngest quarterback to lead his team to a Super Bowl victory. If this doesn't demonstrate the importance of being prepared, what will?

At hedge funds, there is no explicit path for assistants to move into a role where they're taking risk. Some people make a career out of being an assistant, never demonstrating the capability or the desire to graduate to the next level. These people can still be extremely valuable, but most deputies ultimately want to trade themselves. Where there are diligence and aggressive patience, opportunity will eventually knock. When it does, you need to be ready.

CHAPTER SIX

HITTING YOUR STRIDE

You've successfully assimilated into the firm's culture and added value to the desk. You've gained a practical understanding of markets and learned how traders think. You were taught the process of assuming risk, even if you weren't yet taking your own positions, and you now grasp the type of analysis a portfolio manager expects to see before the implementation of a new strategy. Most importantly, you have an appreciation of how the investors and managers want the fund to make money.

You are now ready to be a trader.

A NEW MINDSET

A shift in thinking needs to occur, because there's a considerable difference between being a reliable analyst—the principal function a deputy provides—and a successful trader. Up until this point, you were evaluated on the service you provided others on the desk. You weren't judged on your ability to generate trading profits. Instead, diligence and thoroughness were rewarded. You learned to check your work, making the extra effort to perform sanity checks on all spreadsheets and analysis. Alas, just because you were a superb assistant doesn't mean you'll excel at taking risk.

Coming up with independent trade ideas is a difficult step for many new traders. They have a tendency to withhold from pulling the trigger until they feel 100 percent sure a trade is right. After all, they're coming from the role of an assistant, where they were required to be absolutely sure their work was correct before they passed it along. Traders have to get comfortable operating with a lower level of confidence. That's why there's risk in trading. If there were no uncertainty, then there'd be no chance to profit, since the market would have already repriced to reflect the inevitable outcome. Therefore, traders are often forced to make decisions without the luxury of a complete analysis, or they run the risk of missing an opportunity. In trading, there's no such thing as 100 percent confidence. There's always a chance of being wrong.

Incoming information—new economic data, fluctuating prices, changing sentiment, breaking news—is constant on the trading floor. But not all data is of equal weight and importance. Some information has absolutely no bearing on whether a trade is going to be a winner or loser. In a situation where time is of the essence, traders can't afford to examine all pertinent material methodically. Rather, they must develop a reliable method to separate the wheat from the chaff and identify the real drivers of a potential trade. It's like a game where contestants must put the pieces of a puzzle together without knowing the picture, and the winner is the person who can guess the image first. Every piece provides an additional detail, but if the contestants wait until all the pieces are laid down to guess, they'll probably lose out to a faster competitor. On the trading floor, the key is to complete enough of the puzzle that you're confident, but not 100 percent sure of the answer. There will be times when you act too early, moving without enough information and guessing wrong, and other situations where you wait too long and miss out on the opportunity.

When traders assess opportunities, they calculate possible outcomes based on a range of market reactions, assigning probabilities to these outcomes and identifying catalysts that could trigger various events. An ability to quickly and accurately synthesize relevant information allows the trader to ascertain the most probable scenarios. Once this happens, the trader can act, hopefully beating other market participants. A person who is too analytical, or is constantly waiting for further verification before making a decision, will miss opportunities. Some individuals can't function under such unpredictable conditions and never successfully transition to the role of trader.

Professionals in other careers face similar situations. In January 2009, US Airways flight 1549, piloted by Chesley "Sully" Sullenberger, took off from LaGuardia Airport in New York. Within 90 seconds, flying at an altitude of just over 2,800 feet, the plane was struck by a flock of Canadian geese. Captain Sullenberger had to decide how to proceed. He could either return to the airport or find somewhere else to land. Relying on instincts and forty-two years of flying experience, he chose to land the plane on the Hudson River, saving all 155 passengers onboard.

He didn't have accurate data when he made his decision, and he certainly had no way of knowing the outcome. After evaluating all the potential risks, he calmly relied on his judgment and chose the path with the highest probability of success and minimal downside if he were wrong. If you saw the *60 Minutes* interview he did after the event, you will undoubtedly agree he is one cool cucumber. I bet Sully would make an excellent trader.

PAPER TRADING: WHAT IS IT GOOD FOR?

Nothing can truly prepare you for this transition, although there are small actions to inch you down the path towards success. For instance, seasoned traders will suggest junior team members "paper trade," which tries to mimic the real experience without exposing the participant to real risk. When junior traders paper trade, they analyze opportunities, monitor risk, use actual market levels that incorporate transaction costs, and keep track of profits and losses as if the trades were done with real money. The only difference is they are fictitious. Sometimes, the mock trades are booked in the actual risk system in test accounts. The idea is to give the rookie the chance to fully engage in the trading process without putting capital at risk. It teaches discipline, appreciation for the role of position sizing, and the identification of trade entry and exit points.

This exercise also teaches inexperienced traders the importance of continuing to monitor and analyze trades after execution. Too often, traders fail to deploy the same diligence in monitoring an existing trade as they do when the trade parameters were first identified. Paper trading allows trainees to uncover where the pre-trade and post-trade analysis went right or wrong. Did market events unfold as anticipated? Did the trade perform as expected when market conditions changed? Were the entry and exits points established at the onset of the trade obeyed?

Nonetheless, paper trading is not real trading. It's a simulation. It tests the trainee's analysis, but it fails to replicate the emotional roller coaster that takes off once actual money and risk come into play.

The start of a new trading calendar is always stressful. The P&L scoreboard is reset to zero. Gains and losses from the previous year are gone. Many traders fear digging themselves into a hole of early losses they won't be able to climb out of. Experienced risk-takers still have this concern, but for the rookie, such concerns come with the worry that they'll lose their opportunity to trade. They still have not proven themselves.

When a new trader first engages with the market, an undeniable—somewhat irrational—fear strikes. If the anxiety persists, it can lead the trader to cut a position too early or not even enter the market at all. Many beginners will sit on their hands, eternally waiting for better opportunities to emerge. The job is about taking calculated risks, not avoiding them. If traders physically and mentally can't take risks, they can't produce profits, which is a problem, since as full-fledged traders, their primary function is to make money.

Reading Internet lists of the "Top Ten Trading Rules" isn't going to help. Some of the famous adages are accurate, but anybody in a position to be trading for a hedge fund or other asset manager should already be fully aware of these so-called rules. Reading *Market Wizards* isn't going to turn you into a trading genius, even if it might provide insights. The problem is that no book can teach you how and when to apply the advice, or instruct you how to consistently abide by the rules when burdened by real emotional stress. You probably wouldn't fly a plane solo for the first time with no experience and nothing more than an instruction manual.

"Cut your losses short." Logical advice, but what does it really mean? John Paulson, the hedge fund manager famous for making billions of dollars by shorting sub-prime mortgages in the housing crisis of 2007, didn't follow the traditional advice of many investors when he suffered massive losses before recording historical gains for himself and his investors.

Contrary to popular opinion, there were many market participants engaged in betting against the housing market. Many of these traders, however, reduced risk and cut their losses too early, missing out on the spectacular gains afforded to those who stuck with the trade. Similarly, many who did manage to stick with the short strategy cut their profits too early and lost the chance to generate the kind of returns Paulson, who rode the trade to its maximum payoff, did.

Was Paulson brilliant or imprudent? Maybe both. He certainly had conviction, but we can also say he didn't follow traditional risk management practices. Emotional responses like loss aversion work to prevent a trader from reducing risk and stick with losing trades, and it can also cause premature risk reduction, preventing them from realizing the full potential of profitable trades.

"Use stop-losses." Another piece of advice that is easier said than done. Establishing a stop-loss and following through on it are not the same thing. Many traders have stop-losses, yet they don't use them, or end up changing the level when it is breached. The challenge is to set a prudent and realistic stop-loss level when the trade is established. Some traders are overly cautious and set a stop-loss that is too tight, which means they aren't even giving themselves a chance to win. Stop-losses for medium or long-term trades triggered by short-term moves are a common mistake for those unfamiliar with random noise in the markets. Other traders place a stop-loss too far from the entry point, skewing the upside versus downside or risk versus reward calculation.

For example, if a trade has 3 units of maximum upside, you wouldn't want to place your stop-loss at a point with 5 units of downside. The proper use of stop-losses depends on multiple factors, including the trade horizon, whether the trade is scaled using multiple entry points, and the volatility of the trade. So, while the advice of using stop-losses is sound, their benefit becomes irrelevant if used incorrectly.

Also, leaving a stop-loss order in electronically traded markets is dangerous. Take the "Flash Crash" of August 24, 2015, when many stocks and ETFs (exchange-traded funds) dropped 20 percent, 30 percent, even 40 percent in value in a matter of seconds as the stock market opened. Most stop-loss orders were triggered, but not executed until a bid was found way below the desired exit price.

"Don't pay attention to the news." It's true; by the time you see something on CNBC or read about it in *The Wall Street Journal*, the markets have already reacted. But not all information from the media is extraneous, and participants have to be aware of events that could impair or alter an investment thesis. Maybe a trader shouldn't listen to the talking heads, but he or she will need to identify those sources and data that are relevant and useful to an ongoing trade. Media outlets are beneficial in that they provide a live assessment of market sentiment. If the anchors and their guests are all talking about the possibility of an event and its likely negative outcome as if it was a certainty, there's a good chance that the worst-case scenario is already embedded in the market.

So-called "experts" on television shouldn't have more credibility than anybody else simply because they appear on a business network. In fact, many of the networks don't want to interview people who correctly highlight the uncertainty inherent in the markets. Rather than a discerning guest who recognizes the possibility for various outcomes, they'd rather have two panelists squaring off, each 100 percent convinced that he or she is right. These days, the networks see themselves more as entertainment sources than providers of unbiased information. Still, as previously stated, traders should survey as many media outlets as possible to gauge market positions and identify potentially crowded trades.

"Be disciplined. Control your emotions." Sorry, while this is probably the most applicable piece of trading advice, they've yet to create a pill to blot out the human biases associated with trading. Unfortunately, the only remedy to effectively control emotions is years of experience.

I've been trading for more than two decades, and I'm still susceptible to emotional biases. The rise in popularity of non-discretionary systematic trading is partly in response to the recognition that human emotions often have an adverse impact on trading performance. Systematic trading follows a predetermined strategy and doesn't allow for human intervention. Trading discipline is coded into the game plan, thereby removing emotions from the decision-making process.

If you want to engage in discretionary trading, on the other hand, you'll need to learn how to respond to emotional biases. First, you need to educate yourself about the different tendencies and anticipate when they may rear their ugly heads. A good place to turn for information is the Social Science Research Network, or SSRN. There are hundreds of well-written research papers on cognitive and behavioral science that can provide an overview of most individual biases. Some of the more common biases are discussed in the next chapter.

Paper trading and reading books will take you only so far. Maturing as a trader is a long process. A mentor suggested to me early in my career that it would take ten years. It sounded like an exaggeration when he said it, but it's true.

EVENTUALLY YOU WILL HAVE TO TAKE THE PLUNGE

Some people never learn how to embrace risk and uncertainty. I witnessed this firsthand during my first assignment at Merrill Lynch in London. This was before the euro, and there were eight dealers on the interest rate swaps desk trading more than a dozen currencies. I was a junior trader at the time, and the head of the desk was "Antonio Moretti," a man who loved taking huge risks.

Moretti needed each trader on the team to make a certain amount of money to meet the firm's annual goal or budget. The entire desk, in aggregate, needed to take a minimum amount of risk if there was any chance of reaching those numbers. Each day, Moretti would get a summary of everyone's positions and P&L. It soon became apparent that the person responsible for trading Dutch guilder swaps never made or lost a lot of money.

From reading the report, Moretti could tell that this trader wasn't taking enough risk, most likely because he feared losing money. Periodically, Moretti would walk over and encourage the young trader, who had only recently been awarded his own book, to take a position, explaining that the success of the desk depended on each trader making substantial moves. He thought this personal plea would free up the novice risk-taker and help him overcome this mental block.

The guy was no slouch. He had excelled as an assistant and came to the desk with superb skills. Management would never have made him the go-to trader in charge of the Dutch guilder swaps business if they weren't confident in his abilities. This wasn't a case of somebody who didn't know the market or didn't have the hard skills to trade.

The pep talk didn't help. The trader continued to insist there weren't any positions he liked, arguing patience was the best course. Meanwhile, the rest of the team members managed to get in and out of the market, capitalizing on frequent interest rate gyrations.

After a couple more weeks of not taking any major positions, a frustrated Moretti approached the trader at 8:00 one morning, not long before the futures market opened. He said, "Today is the day you take some risk. I don't care if you make money, and I don't care if you lose money. But by the time the market closes, you had better be up $1 million or down $1 million. Honestly, I don't give a fuck. I just want to see some damn P&L."

The fear in the young trader's eyes was painfully visible to the rest of us on the floor. He was not thinking, "What if I make $1 million?" Rather, he was thinking, "What if I lose $1 million?"

The market opened, and he started trading, but he was still cautious. He couldn't bring himself to take sizable enough positions to hit either end of the target, even with the head of the desk giving him *carte blanche*. He wasn't even close. He lasted another month on the desk before losing his seat to somebody who felt comfortable assuming risk.

A trader is required to embrace risk, not avoid it. I've seen many excellent assistants who had trouble dealing with the authority to make risk decisions, a deficiency they're unaware of until they are placed in that situation.

OVERCOMING YOUR FEAR OF RISK

It's human nature to fear uncertainty, and the investment business is chock-full of unpredictable outcomes. It's common, therefore, for all people, including experienced traders, to have some aversion to risk. It's not the act of trading that creates anxiety, but the fear of the consequences of losing money. Even though the fear is understandable, an overly worried person isn't well suited for a trading career. On the other hand, discovering you're nervous to take on risk once you start doesn't mean you're not cut out for trading. Some anxiety and apprehension are expected, and there are ways to avoid ending up like the guy on the Dutch guilder swaps desk.

Fear of risk can be countered in the same way people deal with common phobias. If someone is afraid of elevators, the remedy isn't for the person to resign him or herself to a lifetime of only taking stairs. Most therapists would recommend confronting the fear to overcome it. The first step is initiating contact with the phobia by standing in front of the elevator. If the person feels calm, he or she can step inside, not to ride, but to feel at ease. Finally, when the person feels safe, he or she can increase exposure by riding it.

Likewise, from a trading perspective, overcoming the fear of losing money entails slow and repeated interaction. It requires losing money and appreciating that it's not unusual, but simply part of the job and expected. If a trader isn't losing money on occasion, he or she isn't trading. What matters is being in control of your losses, so they don't compound and get out of hand.

One way to deal with the anxiety of putting on a trade is to find comfort in a process. A plan consists of knowing what instruments you will trade, when you will enter the market, and what will cause you to exit. A detailed game plan helps you overcome the worry of what to do next.

Trade light, at first. If you operate in the futures market, trade one futures contract instead of a hundred. This will introduce you to the emotional elements of taking risk, and help you practice risk management without the potential for large-dollar losses. Early on, emotions will get the better of you and modest positions will prevent costly drawdowns. As you gain better control over your emotions, your appetite for market exposure will increase, and so will your position sizes.

COST TRADING

Cost trading is one of the bigger mistakes made by new players in the business. It's when the trade entry point becomes the determining factor for deciding the trade exit. I hear it all the time: "If the market ever gets back to where I bought that stupid stock, I'll sell it immediately." Or, "I don't want to lock in a loss. I'm going to wait until the market gets back to my entry point."

Here is an example: A trader buys a stock at $40, and it subsequently drops to $36 over the next week. The stock languishes around the $36 mark for a few more days, casting doubt on the original thesis. The trader starts to worry about the mark-to-market loss and pledges to cut the position if the stock gets back to $40. The stock then begins to creep higher. The moment the stock gets back to $40, the trader sells the entire position. That's cost trading.

News flash: The market doesn't know, or care, whether you bought the stock at $40 or $30. The purchase price shouldn't factor into any calculations. Once the stock goes down to $36, the money is lost. Check the P&L statement if you don't believe me. The only question you should ask is, "Where does the stock go from $36?" Maybe the fundamentals have changed, in which case it could keep dropping, making the decision to sell the right choice. Hoping that it will go back up to $40 without any data to back up such a projection is pure gambling. Hope isn't a strategy. As the saying in the business goes, "If you're hoping and wishing, cut that position."

Another possibility is you still like the stock at $36 for all the same reasons you bought it at $40 and you decide to hang on. If you were paper trading, you'd probably see the drop as a possibility to buy more at a lower level. The approach should be identical with real capital. A well-developed, professional trader understands he or she is mark-to-market daily. Where the stock is going from its current point is all that matters. What you paid for the stock shouldn't factor into your decision whether to hold, buy more, or sell.

You can avoid cost trading if you plan your exit at the same moment you decide on your entry. Plan your profit target, stop-loss, and a location where you'd add more to the trade. Of course, you will only reap the benefits of a plan if you stick to it. You need to be extraordinarily disciplined.

Many seasoned operators scale in and out of trades rather than committing to buy or sell a security at one given price. Scaling is the same as averaging—multiple trades, of the same or similar sizes, done in the same security at various levels. Scaling can be deployed both if the position is going against you or in your favor. The likelihood of picking the exact top or bottom is minuscule, so traders often average into a position to avoid getting stopped out too early. Stop-losses can be set as a dollar amount in addition to a price target. This is an effective risk management technique that also prevents psychological anchoring to a single price-point.

Don't be too hard on yourself. You're never going to be right 100 percent of the time, and you're rarely going to be able to buy at the bottom and sell at the top. In the last twenty years, I've picked the exact bottom and sold at the peak on only a handful of occasions. Every other time, I've had to deal with being either too early or too late. And in the few lucky situations where I did manage to round trip a trade from the absolute bottom to the top, I ended up beating myself up for mis-sizing the trade and not doing enough!

The longer I'm a pupil of the markets, the greater appreciation I gain for the impact of psychological influences on trading and investing. When I first started, I viewed the game as me against the market. Now, I consider the game as me against other people. The more you comprehend the positions of other traders and investors, and how they might react in certain situations, the better chance you have of predicting market movements. Identifying the consensus view and how other participants are positioned in various trades has become one of my most important evaluation criteria.

When people think of a trading pit, they often think of the famous scene from the film *Trading Places* in which Eddie Murphy and Dan Aykroyd make a killing in the orange juice—"OJ"—futures pit. Rumors of an OJ shortage send prices skyrocketing before the release of the crop report, with all the traders scrambling to buy futures. The only sellers to emerge at the peak of the frenzy are Valentine and Winthorpe, the characters played by Murphy and Aykroyd. To put it simply, they are selling into a crowd that desperately wants to be long OJ futures.

When the crop report is finally released, it states there is no shortage of orange juice and production is at normal levels. OJ futures plunge from $1.42 per pound to $0.29

per pound, financially destroying the rest of the pit. The only buyers in the crash are Valentine and Winthorpe, who make millions in profit.

Although a fictional scene in a movie, it deftly displays the importance of market positioning and captures the behavioral bias known as herding. It's observable in the old-style, open, outcry futures pits, but it's also relevant to any market where trading occurs. There are a finite number of buyers and sellers, and if traders are over-weighted on one side or the other, the path of least resistance leads into the weight. There's an old market saying describing this phenomenon: "The market tends to move in the direction to screw the most people."

For every buyer there is a seller, but not all players have the same entry point in the market. Nor do they have the same time horizon or capacity to trade. In the OJ pit situation described above, the trading was speculator against speculator with no trading from hedgers (OJ suppliers). As the buyers got long and more aggressive by buying more and more futures at higher and higher prices, they forced the traders who were selling to cover and cut their loss, further driving up the contract value. Eventually, a majority of the traders in the pit were long, and the only shorts were Valentine and Winthorpe. When the buyers wanted to start locking in their profit, in response to the unexpected crop report, there was nobody with the appetite to buy. They all tried to simultaneously sell and caused the price to crash, until Valentine and Winthorpe covered their short position.

This is an excellent example of how markets are inefficient and are subject to a short-term psychological mindset. Psychology and market positioning can drive a market up or down without any material change to fundamentals. It's counterintuitive to want to trade against the crowd, because the crowd can provide momentum to a trade. The problem with trading with the crowd is evident when momentum changes or some sort of external event impacts the market. In this situation, you can get caught needing to trade in the same direction as everybody else—a recipe for sharp price adjustments.

It's always a good idea to ask yourself questions relating to market positioning before you enter a trade, and continually monitor the trade for signs of crowding and consensus opinion. Who else is in the trade? How big is the trade for most people? Do the other people have a short-term or a long-term trade horizon? Where do you think the stop-out points lie for the trade?

Building relationships and communicating with other market participants will help you get answers to some of these questions. Scanning hedge fund holding reports for positions and sizes and evaluating regularly published sentiment indicators and technical analyses are other ways to quantify the degree of crowding. Going with the herd isn't always wrong, but it does often expose your trading to more volatility when the herd shifts direction.

DEVELOPING YOUR OWN STYLE

Muhammad Ali and George Foreman. Two championship boxers with unique styles. Ali used his natural quickness to dance around the ring, mostly staying away from his opponent and striking from the outside. Foreman, on the other hand, was an old-fashioned slugger, relying on his brute strength to end fights with a single punch. Their styles reflected their personal strengths.

Similarly, there are different styles of traders. Some people are aggressive, trading frequently but in a disciplined fashion to capture small movements in the market. Other individuals are patient, only engaging in trades when they believe the market will move significantly, or when they're convinced they have an advantage. Some traders will jump in when they think they have a 55 percent probability of being correct, and others will enter only when the probability of success is perceived to be greater than 80 to 90 percent. Some rely solely on market technicals or price action to decide whether or not to buy or sell, while others prefer to use fundamental inputs like economic data or earnings reports. No two traders are exactly alike, and it's absolutely critical to develop a style consistent with your beliefs, personality, and individual strengths.

Your personal convictions are indispensable, because they underpin your fundamental view of how markets operate. For example, do you believe in the efficient market hypothesis, which states that all information related to a security or market is accurately reflected in its price? Or, do you think markets are inefficient and prices can temporarily move away from their fair value? Your opinion on this subject will play a major role in how you approach investing.

Personality also plays a significant role in your optimal trading style or strategy, as discussed earlier. Depending on your propensity for risk, volatility, and stress, some styles of trading will be more suitable than others. A good relative value trader may not be a good directional trader, and vice versa. Naturally, as an assistant, you'll be influenced by the style of the senior member on the desk, but when you transition to full-time trading, you'll need to develop your own method.

There are many forms of trading. Each one deploys different tactics and plays into different personality traits.

The following styles can be combined and are relevant to all time horizons. For example, you can have short-term directional systematic approach, or a long-term discretionary relative value one.

- **Momentum:** Buying or selling a security after the price has an established trend, either up or down, with increasing volume. Example: Buying a stock after it hit its 52-week high on high volume.

- **Mean Reversion:** Taking a position in a security, or securities, that has moved away from its historical trading norm with the expectation the security will eventually revert to its average value. Example: Selling a utilities sector ETF because it's 3 standard deviations rich to its six-month historical average.

- **Directional:** Taking a position in a single asset, using either fundamental or technical data—or both—with the expectation it will rise or fall. Example: Buying crude oil futures at $50 with the opinion that the price will rise.

- **Relative Value:** Taking a long position in a security considered cheap in value and a corresponding short position in a similar, often correlated, security deemed to be relatively rich. This is similar to Mean Reversion. Example: Buying a specific 8-year US Treasury bond and simultaneously establishing a short position in the 10-year bond futures contract with the view the 8-year bond will out-perform the bond future.

- **Systematic:** Trading by way of pre-defined computer models with no human intervention. Example: Buying a stock because the 50-day moving average crossed above the 200-day moving average, which is a buying signal for the automated trading system being utilized.
- **Discretionary:** Trading without sole reliance on statistical models or algorithms. Success is based on the skill of the trader. Example: Selling S&P futures before the US Labor Department's Employment Report, expecting the market to drop once the report is released.

The first head trader I worked for was a character. I would describe him as a perpetual bear, meaning he'd love to trade the market from the short side. We were trading fixed income, specifically Italian government bonds, and he took his biggest positions when going short, meaning he would bet on interest rates going up and the value of bond futures going down. This was raw directional trading. His style and technique naturally influenced the rest of the traders on the team, including me.

I tried and failed, repeatedly, at taking directional exposure. Even when I kept the trading size small, I'd consistently exit at the first sign of a loss, cost trade, and monetize gains too quickly when I had them. It simply was not my style. Getting the timing right was critical, and, for whatever reason, it wasn't suited to my personality. The head trader and I could be looking at the identical set of data, and his filters would locate the right circumstances to trade, while my filters and analysis wouldn't lead me to the same conclusions.

Over the years, this trader had developed an effective process to complement his preferred style and personality. He wasn't afraid of taking big losses, and he appeared to have a high tolerance for stress. The filters he used to initiate trades worked for him, as did his emotional response to the volatility associated with directional trading. It's possible I would've found success had I stuck to this style and worked at developing more efficient filters and better emotional control, but the early negative feedback discouraged me, and I never located a passion for this particular method.

Trading style is also molded by past experience. The chief risk-taker described above is a perfect example. He began trading Italian bonds known as BTPs during a period of massive volatility stemming from substantial fiscal problems in Italy. Due to the political and economic instability, bond prices were susceptible to large, sudden downward movements. When they did go up in value, they tended to do so much more gradually. His trading style was to wait for the right set-up to position for a drop in prices, to capitalize on what he thought would be an out-sized move to the downside. Early on, his style developed from the way the BTP market traditionally behaved, and he stuck with it through his entire trading career.

By the time I started trading on the desk, the Italian government bond market was beginning to change. There was no longer the same downside volatility, due to expectations of a European Monetary Union. The idea of economically linking eleven countries in Europe with a common currency meant interest rates and credit risk would be curtailed going forward, or, at least, materially lower than their historical norms. Nevertheless, to his detriment, the trader clung to his style of trading from the short side. Not all styles are profitable in every situation.

The trader from the previous chapter who questioned our mandate and wanted us to abandon our relative value approach by going long credit is another example of the market environment influencing a trading style. His focus was so narrow because, in his brief experience in the industry, all he had seen were credit spreads tightening. His limited experience made him believe credit spreads moved in only one direction and the surest way of making money was to bet on the continuation of the trend.

The conscious or subconscious impact of market conditions on trading style is understandable. The easiest way to make money in the short term, after all, is to go with the trend. Participants who enter the industry during an equity bull market are often predisposed to trade from the long side. Similarly, those who start during a bear market are more comfortable trading from the short side. For example, a majority of interest-rate dealers on Wall Street today are young and have never witnessed a bear market in bonds. Their view, shaped by a decade marked by 0 percent policy rates and central bank quantitative easing, is that interest rates only decline and are naturally supposed to remain low. They've never traded through a tightening cycle. People worry about what would happen if interest rates rose dramatically and central bank support were withdrawn. Would they know how to handle a market going through such a regime change?

Some styles limit the psychological biases associated with relying solely on either long or short selling strategies. Momentum trading is an example. In this style, traders are agnostic to market direction and look to profit from substantial moves in either direction. Price action and volume determine their trading signals. Accelerating price movement, up or down, on strong volume, indicates positive momentum. As it happens, this approach was not a natural fit for me either.

When I was in London, the head of the interest rate derivatives business had his own proprietary trading book. Periodically, he'd trade to offset the risk of the various desks if he felt one particular exposure was too large for the business. Other times, he'd use the account to express his personal view. He'd prance over to the trading desk after the release of an instrumental piece of economic data wanting to establish a large direction position after the market had already had a massive move.

To me, it seemed counterintuitive. Why buy or sell something that had already moved considerably? Wasn't the market overbought or oversold? Wouldn't it be better to try to fade the move and wait for a better entry? His mentality was that the market had materially changed and momentum was on his side, meaning it was the right circumstances to add to the trade, not reduce.

Part of the difference in our outlook came down to how long both of us expected to hold the trade. He was looking at it as a money-making opportunity over the next three months. All I could see was the position getting killed in the next three days as people took profits. The inevitable market pullbacks made me feel uneasy, even if they'd only be temporary. I have always had difficulty buying higher highs and selling lower lows, which is an issue successful momentum players must overcome.

A three-month stint in Toronto as part of the Merrill Lynch training program exposed me to systematic trading, which also turned out to be unsuitable for my personality. Systematic trading deploys computer models, primarily based on technical analysis of market data or statistics, to identify and trade with little or no trader intervention. One of the traders on the desk in Toronto had developed a system to signal whether to buy or sell short-term interest-rate volatility. His method was purely systematic and nondiscretionary. When the model said buy, he bought. When the model said sell, he sold. It usually worked for him, but it didn't make any intuitive sense to me. I could never commit capital simply on the basis of a model signal, ignoring all other factors outside of the model inputs. My personal style required a better explanation of why volatility might be out of line, and why it was likely to revert back to normal. To deploy any effective systematic strategy requires 100 percent belief in the system and process, combined with complete discipline in its implementation. In this case, such standards were clearly absent for me.

Some of the most successful hedge fund managers in the world are systematic traders. Juggernauts like Renaissance Technologies have built elaborate quantitative systems with outstanding performance records. Computers and software at such institutions analyze and calculate gigabytes of data every day—or every minute—to crank out trades with a slight edge. There is no possible way for humans to process this volume of data. Another added benefit to systematic strategies is that they remove the emotional element of trading. The models don't suffer from greed or fear.

The industry certainly seems to be moving in the direction of more systematic trading strategies. It's a style that requires a heavy quantitative background and a full release of discretionary oversight. Personally, I have difficulty handing over 100 percent discretion to a model, despite being cognizant of the benefits of taking out of the equation human emotions and the poor decisions they generate.

Ultimately, your trading style or method may come down to the luck of where you land. Sometimes, you don't have a choice in how you would like to trade. If you find a position at a hedge fund that specializes in one particular style of trading, they'll probably be unwilling to experiment with alternative methods. This highlights the need to do your due diligence when evaluating investment firms to try to find the right match.

As stated earlier, my previous attempts at directional trading proved to be too emotionally taxing. Consequently, when I moved to the prop desk at UBS in London, I focused on the lower stress style of relative value trading, or RV. RV trading uses a combination of fundamentals and statistics to identify relationships in the market that appear mispriced compared to their historical norms. In some ways, it's the opposite of momentum trading, where traders capitalize on a move already underway. When I got a lucky break and joined my existing hedge fund, the fact that they focused exclusively on RV, at the time, made them a perfect match. Finding the right fit translated into greater interest in and passion for my work. It also gave me greater confidence when it came to trading.

STICK TO THE PLAN

Fidelity to style, especially during drawdown periods, is of paramount importance. Imagine you're a baseball player, and you finally get the call to the majors. Right from the start, you're hitting, showing good power and patience at the plate. After a couple of weeks, however, you fall into a slump. You can't buy a hit. Even the hardest struck balls seem to find the fielders' gloves. You start wondering if you're ever going to start hitting again. Self-doubt begins to creep into your mindset. Maybe you were lucky through college ball and the minors, but now the major league pitchers have you figured out, and you'll never have much of a major league career. You start pressing at the plate, swinging at pitches way out of the zone. The hitting coach pulls you aside. He explains that every player goes through slumps, and the only way to break it is to stick to the process. Now is not the time to tinker with your batting stance. Don't try to hit the ball too hard or pull it. Wait for your pitch—it will come—and the ball off your bat will start finding gaps.

The slump analogy applies to trading. In trading, when you go through a bad period, namely a string of losing trades, the only option is to stay in the game. Don't abruptly change your trading style. Instead, stick to your process, assuming it has brought you some degree of success in the past. Tinkering with your process will only add doubt to your trading and reduce your confidence. Don't try to recoup prior losses by doing trades you wouldn't normally do. Instead of stopping all trading, reduce your standard size during this period. I have reduced my average position size by as much as 90 percent until my performance improved, and I regained my confidence.

Moreover, this is an excellent opportunity to review the trades responsible for the losses, since it's possible the slump is related to a breakdown of discipline in your decision-making. Professional trading coaches advise their clients to keep a detailed log of all their trades and their analysis. The discipline of documenting all this data can sometimes help identify breakdowns unknown to the trader.

Fortunately, in most instances, you'll eventually be able to identify a slump as just that, a temporary setback. The more you've been in and out of trading slumps, the more you'll recognize they are simply part of risking money in the markets. While every setback is painful, you'll gain confidence in the fact that sticking to your process is the only way to emerge intact.

At some funds, if traders are in a lengthy slump, and they will not cut back on their own, the portfolio manager is forced to intervene. Essentially, the traders' ability to take risk is removed for a period, maybe a week, a month, or even longer. During this period, the traders are expected to keep following the market. It's a mental reset button to remove the biases and negative emotions affecting performance and confidence. Every firm has its method of dealing with individuals who are going through a losing streak, but traders are better off identifying the problem on their own and taking appropriate steps to address the issue before the risk department steps in.

MATURING AS A TRADER

Successful trading doesn't hinge solely on market analysis. It greatly depends on self-awareness or the trader's comprehension of his or her unique personality and biases. The mechanical skills in trading can be developed relatively quickly; the mental skills take time. In other words, there is a steep learning curve for trading IQ, but a much slower curve for trading EQ.

I recently was invited into a hockey locker room where an NHL sports psychologist was hired to address a team of 20-year-old up-and-coming players. It was the start of the season, and the coach was determined to give his team an advantage.

The psychologist started the session with a question. "How many of you think there's a mental aspect to peak performance on the ice?" As you might expect, every player's hand went up.

He followed with another question. "Then, what percentage of the game is mental?"

"Twenty-five percent," answered one. "Fifty percent," said another. "One hundred percent," the coach shouted from the back of the room.

The psychologist's next comment left the room in silence. "It appears it's somewhere between 25 percent and 100 percent. Now, how many of you spend the same amount of time working on improving your mental game as you do improving your physical game?"

Hands stayed down. Despite recognizing the mental aspect of the sport, the players had not put any thought into how they could improve this part of their game. They probably didn't even know where to start.

Successful traders are similar. They acknowledge their mental approach is responsible for a large part of their performance. After all, trading is about making sound decisions, and emotions often cloud our decision-making process. Recognizing and controlling negative emotions, therefore, is crucial. Yet little effort is placed on identifying mental strengths and weaknesses.

The emergence of behavioral finance as a discipline has helped investors put a name to the biases they possess. While the leading theorists in this field may not be household names outside the world of finance, people like Daniel Kahneman and Richard Thaler have made a material contribution toward improving the understanding of various biases in investing.

Common cognitive biases investors struggle to overcome:

THE ENDOWMENT EFFECT: ascribing more value to a stock merely because you own it.

ANCHORING: judging that a stock price is overvalued or undervalued based on that stock's previous high or low share price.

CONFIRMATION BIAS: seeking out information that validates existing beliefs and opinions.

HERDING: following the masses with the view that the crowd is always right.

OUTCOME BIAS: evaluating a trade or investment based on its outcome rather than the quality of the decision.

FRAMING: drawing contrasting conclusions from the same information depending on how that information is presented.

RECENCY BIAS: the most recent news, information, or price action plays a bigger role in decision-making than historical information or price action.

These biases have been present for a long time, although, like the hockey players described above, most professional traders do nothing to address them, subjecting themselves to the same mistakes over and over again. Let's take confirmation bias as an example. There's a tendency for investors to seek out and accept narratives that support their current view and positioning in the market. Articles arguing against their current outlook are often dismissed as irrelevant, unimportant, or outright wrong. New material isn't analyzed with the same unbiased intensity as the information present when the trade thesis was formed.

Confirmation bias happens when traders are "married" to their positions. The solution to dealing with the bias is simple: establish a rigorous system of analysis that seeks to validate both sides of potential and existing investments, regardless of predetermined beliefs or existing positions, and continue to do so as information changes or evolves.

Behavioral biases are present in traders and investors, but that doesn't mean you can't take steps to minimize their effects. One remedy, if you find yourself subject to a behavioral bias, is to exit the trade, regardless of whether the position is making or losing money. Of course, sometimes this is not practical. But if it can be accomplished, you'll likely find yourself suddenly liberated from your emotions and thinking clearer. Starting with "a clean sheet of paper," the position can be reestablished the next day after a fundamental and technical review. (Choosing not to restore the trade is an indication that certain biases were indeed at play.)

BUILDING RELATIONSHIPS, BUILDING TRUST

When people outside the industry think about trading, they generally don't think of it as a relationship business. However, when you're not spending your time watching the market, you're building relationships. You may be speaking with an economist or developing new trade ideas with other members of your team. Depending on the products you deal with, you could be talking to your liquidity providers—the individuals you use to execute your trades.

The relationships you create and foster can play a major role in your success as a trader. There are few trading gigs where you are left alone all day, never speaking to anybody, only executing transactions with the click of a mouse. If you are trading over-the-counter (OTC) products, you'll have to communicate with another person to get a trading level. Examples of OTC markets include fixed-income derivatives, corporate bonds, custom equity derivatives, and unlisted stocks. There is no central exchange to electronically trade these markets, and the price you get is highly dependent on the dealer you call for execution.

During the summer of 2003, I was trading US Treasury asset swaps for the hedge fund where I still work today. Primarily, I was looking for government bonds that were mispriced relative to the interest rate swap curve. At that time, the bond market was becoming concerned with escalating global growth, and 10-year bond yields rose rapidly, increasing by more than 130 basis points over several weeks. The abrupt move in interest rates triggered a wave of activity in the mortgage market. Mortgage investors had a problem. The average life, or duration, of a mortgage increases as interest rates increase, because homeowners have less economic incentive to refinance. The result was massive interest rate hedging by mortgage players to deal with the duration extension. The hedging activity took place in the swap market and created a large dislocation between swap rates and government bond rates. The difference between the two rates is known as the "swap spread."

I was positioned on the winning side of this trade when interest rates rose and the swap spread grew larger. We started making a lot of money as the bond sell-off deepened and the spread moved wider. Swap spreads are not like stocks, which are mostly traded electronically and anonymously. Rather, they are OTC derivative contracts and I needed to find somebody to trade with to get in and out of a position.

One day, during a period of significant volatility, the head of the swaps desk at a major Wall Street bank, a colleague of mine from early in my career, called me. We had a long-standing relationship, and there was an element of trust between us. The market panic was approaching the worst point of the day, and he was on the wrong side of the market. He suspected I had the position he wanted to cover, because he knew our firm had bilateral swap contracts with his bank on the other side to his losing trades. He called looking for help. To reduce his risk, he wanted me to unwind over $1 billion of our 10-year swap spread position.

There was no liquidity anywhere. One would think the immediate reaction would be for me to say, "Thanks, but no thanks," hang up the phone, and trade ahead of the flow, knowing they were going to push the market even further as they sought to cover their position. Surprisingly, that's not what happened.

In any event, I'd been thinking it was a good opportunity to book profits and exit the trade, a fact he probably recognized. In a matter of minutes, we agreed on a fair price and the deal was done. Before he hung up the phone, he said, "Garth, I owe you one," a promise that doesn't mean much, especially when coming out of the mouth of most Wall Street traders.

Sure enough, the market continued to worsen, meaning I had gotten out of the position a little early. Our position could have made several million more dollars had I hung onto it for a a while longer. However, by the end of the day, the trading circus was over, and swap spreads reverted to a more normal state. If I'd not made the deal at that moment, I may have rode spreads up, and then all the way back down.

Several months later, we were in another high volatility situation, and the roles were reversed. Now, I was the one who needed to find a liquidity provider to execute a trade. I called the usual dealers at the other banks to gauge interest and nobody was willing to provide a quote. So, I picked up the handset and called my friend at the bank who "owed me one."

I told him I needed to do a trade almost identical to our previous one, except this time I was the one asking for a favor. At first, there was silence on the other end of the phone. It was clear he was going to lose money on the trade, just like I'd lost some when I'd helped him out months before. After about thirty seconds, he gave me a mid-market price for the trade. Trading at mid-market, the level right in the middle of the quoted bid-ask spread, during such volatility was indeed a favor, since it would have been near impossible to find anybody else to quote me any level at all. I said, "Done." He replied, "We're even."

Hanging up the phone, I was happy that I'd found liquidity in a market where there was none to be found. But I was even more pleased that my counterpart at the bank had honored his word and our business relationship.

Because of that relationship, I managed to achieve an almost impossible trade that allowed me to reduce my exposure. To me, it's a story of the importance of cultivating trust and relationships with everyone you come across in the industry.

I, like many other traders, have other stories about being able to get the liquidity I needed only because of a personal relationship. At the end of the day, if you're trading OTC, you're not trading with the market, but with other people. There's always someone else on the other side of the trade, and when the trade is bilateral, as opposed to electronic, there's an element of trust involved.

Unfortunately, some people enter each trade with the mentality of needing to win in every interaction. I've always tried to approach trading from the perspective that both parties can emerge stronger. A good trade isn't one where you prevent the person on the other side from making money, or cause them to lose significant amounts. When you trade OTC, you're negotiating, and who wants to negotiate with somebody that is always trying to get the best of you? You're not going to succeed in the business if your only method of generating profits is running over the people you transact with. If I'd taken a predatory approach throughout my career, the trades with the dealer described above would never have happened.

If you are constantly emphasizing fairness toward your counterparty, rather than trying to maximize your gain on every single trade, relationships will come back to help you, not haunt you.

One well-known investor worked for a large mutual fund that was the biggest trading account for many of the banks. The fund—especially the head trader—was notorious for running people over and not giving dealers a chance to make money. He would call one minute before the employment numbers were released, a period when all activity usually stops, and demand liquidity for a trade. The bank would reluctantly acquiesce because he was a major client. If they failed to provide liquidity they'd be "put in the box," meaning the fund would temporarily suspend trading with that bank.

Eventually, this trader left the fund and went to work for a much smaller firm. He tried pulling the same maneuver with his trading counterparts, but he had created so much ill will at his previous shop that many of the banks wouldn't even quote him prices, let alone the best ones. Now, when he calls looking to trade minutes before the employment numbers are released, there's nothing but the sound of crickets on the other end of the line. People are not about to help this man, and their reluctance makes it difficult for him to trade the way he wants.

There have been instances when I needed to act shrewdly towards other counterparties, and the actions I took caused them to lose a significant amount of money. Rather than telling the person to suck it up and deal with it, I always apologized and worked to find a way to pay the person back. I went to great lengths to avoid burning bridges. If you don't have trust and integrity with everyone in the business, from the people in the back office up to counterparties at other banks, then there'll be nobody to help when you need a favor, which you'll eventually require at some point in your trading career.

EVERYBODY IS A SALESPERSON

Your official title may say "Trader," but a significant part of the job for many people is sales. As stated earlier, most traders are not isolated in a corner office, staring at their screens while an algorithm automatically executes electronic trades. Although certain situations can be hands off, the majority of trading roles require an element of sales.

If you're a market maker on Wall Street, much of your duty is to create "flow" for your trading book. That means finding customers to trade with. Market makers often find themselves with positions they want or need to get off their balance sheet. In fact, many banks apply additional capital charges to those with stale positions. Therefore, trading operations rely on the salespeople to speak with their clients to generate flow.

Wall Street salespeople serve two masters. They have to help the trading desk get in and out of positions, while at the same time they are obligated to help their clients. Good salespeople want to protect their customers from bad trades, and they won't present a trade to a client unless they truly believe it is appropriate and the price is fair. The trader, therefore, has to sell the idea to the salesperson, convincing him or her that the trade is positive for the client, and in many cases, better than the ideas the other traders want him or her to show. In essence, the trader is competing for the attention of the salesperson.

Hedge fund traders also need to excel at sales. Most traders at hedge funds need to get some involvement from the fund portfolio manager before they execute a trade. If the portfolio manager doesn't like the idea, or doesn't share the same view, the trade won't be put into the fund portfolio. Again, the trader must successfully sell his or her idea to get something done. A good trader knows how to deal with possible objections from a portfolio manager. Some portfolio managers want to see a five-page in-depth write up of a strategy before it is executed, while others will want a five-minute verbal briefing followed by a brief question and answer session.

Appreciating the team element of trading will not only make you a more valuable colleague, but it will help prepare you for the next stage in your career, where relationships are even more crucial.

CHAPTER SEVEN

CONTINUING TO THRIVE

For many on the investing side of the hedge fund business, the long-term goal is to be the person who gets to call the shots. Assistants, analysts, and even most traders are subject to the control of the portfolio manager, or PM. The PM has ultimate discretion over what goes into the portfolio and the size of individual trades.

Some people never transition from trader to portfolio manager. We have traders at our company who've been trading for fifteen years with no aspirations to jump to the next level. They understand there's an additional skill set involved that may not be the right fit for them. They're satisfied, even excited, spending their days on the floor engaged in the mechanics of assembling individual trades. Moving to the next level comes down to desire, but it also depends on old-fashioned luck. Sometimes a failure to advance is attributable to the simple fact that there may be no available openings. At most hedge funds, the ratio of traders to PMs is quite high. There may be five to ten traders for every PM. Also, a successful portfolio manager, who is often the founder of the firm, can stay in the position for many years, preventing upward mobility for those aspiring to gain more responsibility.

There is no single path someone must follow to move from trading to the portfolio management function. It can happen in a variety of ways, similar to how assistants transition into full traders. The business can open additional funds or an existing PM could retire, get fired, or move to a competitor. In some cases, the only path for you to become a PM may involve moving to another shop, or even starting your own.

AN INCH DEEP AND A MILE WIDE

Most people outside of the industry aren't aware of the difference between traders and PMs. At smaller hedge funds, the roles of PM and trader are often held by the same person. In larger enterprises, however, the PM function is different from that of a trader and requires a distinct skill set.

A trader's function is to design, develop, and execute trading strategies for a particular market. For example, if you're responsible for trading US Treasury Bonds, the vast majority of your effort should be spent on becoming an expert in all aspects of the US government bond market. You have to follow investment flows, central bank policy, regulatory developments, bond issuance patterns, and so on. At sell-side firms, there may be five to ten independent traders on the government bond desk, resulting in an even narrower focus for each individual. There is often a single person specializing in the 2-year sector, and another who only trades bonds with maturities of around 10 years. They don't trade anything else, and they know their markets like the back of their hand. The more knowledge the trader has in a specific area, the more he or she can access and understand the relevant data and identify trading opportunities. In these situations, one can say, a trader swims in a lane that is an inch wide and a mile deep.

The opposite is true for most portfolio managers. They need to operate in a lane that is an inch deep and a mile wide. They're required to be knowledgeable about multiple markets and have the ability to synthesize a vast amount of information into actionable investment decisions. PMs decide the what, when, why, and how of all ideas in the portfolio. Ultimately, the responsibility for the performance of the fund rests with the PM.

The relationship between the PM and the traders is similar to the relationship between an architect and a custom homebuilder. The architect designs a house in accordance with the needs and desires of the client. Then, he or she works with the builder to implement a detailed plan consistent with various building codes. A good architect is knowledgeable about the construction process and will not ask the builder to do the impossible. A good builder, on the other hand, will provide valuable feedback to the architect about elements of the design that may be cost prohibitive or impractical to implement. A close relationship between the architect and the builder is required to deliver the end product successfully.

At a hedge fund, the PM is the architect and the traders are the builders. The PM designs the portfolio, ensuring the exposures are consistent with the mandate provided by the investors. The traders use their expertise to execute the chosen trades in the most efficient manner possible. They give feedback to the PM on what is achievable and what could potentially cause problems. In some cases, they work with the PM to find an alternative solution or trade construction. The PM decides what risks to take, and the traders' role is to determine the optimal implementation, considering criteria like transactions costs, liquidity, and the need for discretion. The relationship hinges on sharing insights and ideas.

While many portfolio managers will come up with their own trades, the primary function of the PM is to aggregate the best ideas from the traders and analysts and decide where to allocate capital. The PM looks at all the trade options and determines where to overweight and where to underweight and, most critically, where to avoid.

Ideas between the PM and traders flow both ways. Traders are constantly showing the PM fresh opportunities for the portfolio that the PM hasn't already identified. The PM will have to determine which trades, if any, fit best. The PM must evaluate which strategies possess the best risk-reward ratio and which risks are already fully expressed in the portfolio. The ultimate goal of the PM is to find a combination of strategies to generate sufficient returns for the fund to meet its performance objective.

In other circumstances, the PM will approach a trader in a specific sector with concepts the PM is trying to develop, asking the trader to identify and structure a trade to capitalize on the anticipated move in the market. It's the responsibility of the trader to present the PM with several alternatives to express the view. The PM will then decide which option is most fitting.

Stress levels are often amplified in the portfolio manager position. When a trader has exposure on the book, it's a stressful period, but the duration of most trades is finite. They could last anywhere from one day to several years, but the trade is eventually removed once it runs its course. Portfolio managers, on the other hand, don't share this advantage. As the individuals responsible for the performance of the fund, there's pressure to continuously have risk in the portfolio. Investors are not hiring them to sit on cash. They expect PMs to always have a current view of the market and a position to match.

Determining the size of a position is another stress that falls on the shoulders of the portfolio manager. For example, a trader responsible for monitoring the energy sector may decide, after running detailed analysis, that Exxon is a strong candidate for outperforming the rest of the industry. The trader presents the PM with three ways to express the view: buy Exxon stock outright, buy Exxon and short the energy sector as a whole, or buy Exxon call options. The portfolio manager is obliged to consider how each trade will impact the rest of the portfolio, and which one has the most upside versus downside, or the best risk-reward ratio.

Keeping score is part of trading. Pundits love to identify round numbers in the stock market with more significance than is due. Meanwhile, traders remember round numbers in a different way. Most institutional traders remember the first time they made or lost $100,000 in a single day. They surely remember when they made or lost $1 million in a single day. I remember when we made $100 million in a single morning.

It was the first quarter of 2008, and the credit crisis was beginning to bubble over. We had recently launched a new fund dedicated to short the credit market, meaning we and our investors would stand to benefit if credit conditions deteriorated and credit spreads widened. Amongst other methods, we expressed the view through buying insurance, also known as credit default swaps, on a basket of 125 separate US companies.

Prior to the crisis, the cost of the insurance for a basket of these investment-grade entities was approximately 50 basis points (bps), or one half of 1 percent a year. We expected the market to factor in additional risk in the credit market that would make the insurance more expensive and provide a profit to our fund.

The price of the insurance, or the spread, started in January at approximately 60 bps. By the beginning of March, it was starting to accelerate higher, with the spread widening to 150 bps. Our position grew to about $2 million per basis point during that period, so we expected to make $20 million in profit for every 10 bps of widening.

Conditions were getting worse, and all hell broke loose one morning in early March 2008. Right before the start of the weakness in January, the typical daily trading range for the trade we had on would be 1 to 2 basis points. It wasn't considered a volatile or risky instrument. As spreads began to widen, however, the trading range got larger. There were times in February when the credit spread would move 5 to 10 bps in a day. On that day in March, the credit spread opened up at 160 bps and quickly gapped higher. By 10:00 in the morning it had exceeded 200 bps.

We began to take profits. As you might imagine, liquidity at this point was quite constrained. There was no price transparency and market makers were reluctant to quote anything. We'd execute a trade, and a moment later the market would move 5 bps in either direction. I can remember the look on the faces of our traders. They were thinking I was crazy for not waiting for more widening.

The trade had run its course, I believed at the time. We needed to book profits while we still had liquidity. We were on the right side of the market. When most players were scrambling to buy insurance, we were one of the few players who had insurance to sell.

At this point, I knew it would be a record P&L day. When all the trades were booked into the system I managed to get a look at the day's tally: $102 million. It was my best day ever, and also one of the most stressful—and memorable—moments in my career.

The decision over which trade to pick will also depend on the trade catalyst, or the event expected to drive performance. Is the view that Exxon will perform better than the industry this week, this quarter, or next year? The answer will help determine the optimal structure. In addition, these decisions will hinge on the overall level of risk presently in the portfolio, impacting the desirability of an outright directional position in Exxon compared to the long/short strategy or the call option. Finally, once a structure is chosen, the critical decision of trade sizing must be considered. How much capital *can* be allocated to this one idea? How much of the available capital *should* be risked on this one idea? How should it be sized in relation to the other market exposures in the portfolio? All of these decisions are determined at the PM level.

Risk for a trader is often one-dimensional. The trader evaluates each opportunity on its own merits, and the idea ultimately turns out to be either good or bad. The portfolio manager, however, must view risk as multi-dimensional. The PM must consider not just the merits of a trade in isolation, but also how it interacts with the rest of the portfolio. Is it additive to risk or risk reducing? How large should one trade be relative to another? What's the overall level of portfolio risk?

Portfolio managers must be cognizant of how various events—both positive and negative—can impact positions. Stress testing is a process that runs the portfolio through various potential market events to gauge the economic consequences of different scenarios, like a global recession, high inflation, deflation, a commodity boom/bust, a debt crisis, or changes in short- and long-term interest rates. Stress testing illuminates the degree of different exposures embedded in the portfolio. Positive and negative returns resulting from the test should be consistent with the economic views of the PM.

SECOND- AND THIRD-ORDER EFFECTS

To perform better than other managers, a PM needs to come up with novel investment ideas. Creative PMs look beyond the obvious and spend a lot of energy thinking

Being a PM is like drinking from a fire hose. The PM must pay attention to a massive amount of rapidly changing information and learn enough about each topic to gauge its importance to the positions in the portfolio. The passage of Dodd-Frank, for example, had a major impact on investment decisions. The PM must understand the impact of such legislation on portfolio positions and make adjustments as needed. Below is a small sample of risks every portfolio manager should be paying attention to, to reduce the risk of getting blindsided by markets.

Economic Concerns:

- Risk of a US recession
- Risk of a global inflation
- Risk of slowdown in emerging markets

Central Bank Policy:

- Impact of changes to federal funds rate
- Likelihood of changes to non-conventional policies like quantitative easing
- Changes to forward guidance

Political Events:

- Impact of elections in various countries
- Regulatory developments
- Changes to domestic tax or trade policy and its potential economic impact

Exogenous Shocks:

- Pandemics
- Natural disasters
- Commodity cycles

Geopolitical Events:

- Role of anti-globalization
- Developments in the Middle East conflict
- Rise of global terrorism

about better ways to structure and implement their views. Earlier in the book, we discussed this idea of second-order effects, which is about considering market developments beyond the market's initial response.

Imagine a scenario where there is an exogenous shock to the markets, like a sudden over-supply of crude oil. The first-order effect is the price of oil falling. A second-order effect could be a widening of credit spreads for oil producers with highly leveraged balance sheets who will have trouble refinancing debt with reduced cash flow. A third-order effect could be a decline in the value of bank shares that have lent a significant amount of money to the energy sector. This would be in anticipation of loan write-downs negatively impacting profits. The primary responsibility of a portfolio manager is to think through the potential impact these three effects will possibly have on the entire portfolio. PMs need to anticipate, not just react. To use another sports metaphor, they need to skate to where the puck is going, not where it has been.

Analyzing multiple markets across a range of products is no easy task, especially in macro strategies where there are few restrictions on where PMs can invest and what instruments they can use to express their ideas. They need a good filter and a consistent process when allocating capital. What is the upside of each strategy if you're

"THE BIGGEST INVESTING ERRORS COME NOT FROM FACTORS THAT ARE INFOR-MATIONAL OR ANALYTICAL, BUT FROM THOSE THAT ARE PSYCHOLOGICAL."

The mental component is huge in trading, as we discussed in the last chapter. The above quote proposes that the greatest sources of opportunity emerge in those periods when everyone else is succumbing to psychological errors. If you can keep your wits about you when everyone else is losing theirs, you can beat the market and profit. What makes Howard Marks a standard bearer of the industry is his ability to wait for favorable opportunities to come along. He preaches patience while acknowledging that waiting on the sidelines is one of the greatest challenges. His talent for knowing when to act aggressively is equal to his awareness of when to display caution.

right? What is the downside of each trade if you're wrong? Is each idea equally liquid? Could the trade structures be altered to improve the upside versus downside ratio? These are some of the questions a PM would need to ask before arriving at a decision, and it's creative thinking that will help a PM through this process.

RISK IS EVERYWHERE

Portfolio managers need to feel comfortable with the idea of constant risk. As mentioned earlier, individual traders operate with certain luxuries that are unavailable to portfolio managers. If a trader were nervous about the impact of some known geopolitical event, major economic data, or change in central bank policy, then he or she could take off any position in advance of the news. A portfolio manager, on the other hand, may have hundreds of positions in the portfolio, and taking them all off isn't a simple, cost-free, efficient move. There would be significant transaction costs and concerns surrounding available liquidity. A fund could lose a substantial amount of money if it were to take the positions off and then put them back on after the event is over. The PM could establish some liquid hedges in the short run, but they're unlikely to remove all residual risks from the portfolio. PMs are rarely "flat," or without any risk.

THERE IS NOTHING CERTAIN ABOUT LIQUIDITY

Broadly defined, liquidity refers to a trader's ability to get in and out of a security. Liquid markets have tight bid-ask spreads. In other words, the percentage difference between where you can buy or sell a security is small. Liquid markets also have observable prices, continuous trading, and high volume.

An example of a liquid market is the S&P 500 Index ETF, ticker symbol SPY. SPY trades over 100 million shares a day, equal to more than $20 billion. This volume, combined with a bid-ask spread of just 1 cent, allows traders to easily get in and out of positions throughout the day.

Illiquid markets have the opposite characteristics—wide bid-ask spreads, non-transparent prices, sporadic trading, and low volume. It's important to note that market liquidity isn't constant. A market can quickly transform from being highly liquid to completely illiquid. When this happens, it can cause a massive amount of disruption to an investment portfolio, as it can prevent a PM from making position adjustments. The PM can't buy to take advantage of a mispricing, nor can he or she sell to reduce risk. Trading can stop completely. Trying to buy or sell anything in a market that has gone from liquid to illiquid can be expensive at best, and impossible at worst.

An example of an illiquid market is the high-yield corporate bond market. Bonds of some issuers trade infrequently, possibly going weeks without trading at all. There is little price transparency and investors can experience difficulty getting a reasonable bid or offer. When the bonds do trade, it may be for just $1 or 2 million, a small amount for an institutional transaction.

Becoming a judicious portfolio manager begins with appreciating that liquidity can change in a heartbeat. A market classified as highly liquid today can be deemed absolutely illiquid tomorrow. The speed at which liquidity dynamics can change brings to mind the famous Hemingway line from *The Sun Also Rises*: "'How did you go

bankrupt?' 'Two ways...Gradually and then suddenly.'"
It can happen without warning in any market.

Liquidity is a trader's lifeblood. In 2008, for example, during the global financial crisis, the ability to trade evaporated in certain markets, paralyzing traders. They couldn't exit trades or deploy stop-losses because nobody was willing or able to take the other side of the trade. Essentially, they lost control of the plane, and rule number one for traders and PMs is to always be in control of the aircraft.

Finding an attractive opportunity in a liquid market is always a short-term trader's best option. Often, however, investors have good reason to enter illiquid markets. With an appropriately long time horizon, sacrificing liquidity for a higher expected return is a sound strategy. The PM is accepting the risk that he or she may have difficulty exiting the position in certain market situations. It would be suicide for a portfolio manager to create an entire portfolio full of illiquid securities, but this doesn't mean it's never a risk worth taking if sized correctly. In fact, the market term for the concept of picking up incremental return in exchange for assuming risk in an illiquid market is known as the "liquidity premium." Using the plane analogy again, a liquid portfolio is like flying a fighter jet, whereas an illiquid portfolio is like flying a B-52 bomber. One is much more maneuverable than the other.

Sometimes you're handsomely rewarded for operating in illiquid markets or securities. Other times, receiving additional expected compensation or return is not worth the risk of being trapped in a trade. The liquidity premium can be tracked historically in most markets, and often moves in cycles that can last years, and as a PM, you need to be aware of where you are in the cycle at any given point to assess whether or not you're getting paid appropriately for taking liquidity risk.

The fund's mandate and terms play a significant role in determining how much a manager will ultimately allocate to illiquid markets. The terms between hedge funds and their investors, after all, are not standardized. For example, if a hedge fund has a three-year lockup period, meaning investors cannot redeem shares during this period, a manager will have greater leeway to invest in illiquid instruments. Still, a manager can only afford so much exposure to these markets if he or she has any intention of being able to trade in and out of positions actively.

On the other hand, if a fund has a thirty-day redemption period, meaning, if asked, it must return the money to investors with one month's notice, then dealing in illiquid securities can come at a high cost, especially if everyone redeems at once. In 2008, many investors in hedge funds hit the panic button and asked for their money back at exactly the same time. This demand forced funds to unwind similar trades in tandem, shattering the equilibrium between buyers and sellers. Prices spiraled downward since there were no buyers to accommodate the numerous sellers.

The concept of avoiding crowded positions and going against the consensus view has already been discussed. One downside of being in a crowded trade is that when illiquidity and volatility erupt you can find yourself competing with other traders to exit positions. With everybody scrambling to trade in the same direction, prices adjust immediately. Conversely, if you're in a situation where you can be the liquidity provider, because you're on the less crowded side of the market, you can usually extract fantastic value from the distressed investors.

With the constant threat of illiquid markets, correct position sizing is critical for a portfolio manager. Suppose a trader, in a liquid environment, accumulated $50 million of a particular corporate bond, buying a market-standard $5 million a clip over the course of several weeks. In this case, it took ten individual transactions to reach the target amount of $50 million. Then one day, maybe after the issuer disclosed an accounting scandal or horribly missed earnings expectations, the PM instructs the trader to exit the position. This former darling of the market, however, was an overweight position in many bond portfolios, and traders at other institutions received similar instructions on the same day.

Because other traders are now trying to exit simultaneously, buyers become more cautious, lowering the quote they'll provide to sellers while also reducing the amount they'll buy at each incremental price level. In this scenario it's possible the average trade size could fall to $1 million per clip. On top of this, the bond trades just once per day, instead of many times per day, as it did when the position was established. It will now take fifty transactions over fifty days to unwind. The price where the PM decided he or she wanted to exit would be dramatically different from the actual price received. What good is a stop-loss level if you can't execute the stop?

A major criticism leveled against large hedge funds is their inability to maneuver in and out of markets. Hedge funds, after all, market themselves on their flexibility and nimbleness. There is no question the largest hedge funds are constrained by size, making it difficult for them to establish and unwind large positions. In fact, there's data to back up the claim that smaller funds outperform larger ones for this exact reason. According to a study conducted by three professors at City, University of London in 2015, larger funds (those in the top decile of assets under management) underperformed smaller funds (those in the bottom decile) by almost 1.7 percent per year between 1995 and 2015.[1]

Smaller funds have position sizes that allow them to maneuver with greater ease and speed. Further, giant funds cannot always take advantage of the best opportunities due to the liquidity in any one security or market.

Some of the best ideas are those where only a finite amount of capital can be deployed. Let's look at the impact of position sizing for a $30 billion bond fund compared to a $30 million fund. Assume both PMs have a policy of allocating a maximum of 5 percent of the firm's capital to their single best idea. For the $30 billion fund, this policy would translate into a $1.5 billion position, compared to a $1.5 million position for the $30 million fund. It's possible to find a bond mispriced by a few points where you could allocate $1.5 million. Finding a mispriced bond where you can commit $1.5 billion is highly unlikely. The larger fund would probably pass on the $1.5 million opportunity, since such a small position in a $30 billion portfolio would have a negligible impact on the fund's overall performance. It would simply be a distraction in terms of risk

---

1   Lawrence C. Strauss, "How Small Hedge Funds Outperform Bigger Rivals," *Barron's*, November 8, 2015, http://www.barrons.com/articles/how-small-hedge-funds-outperform-bigger-rivals-1448691462.

management and would not move the needle with respect to performance.

Superior PMs are aware of the trade-off between maintaining liquidity and seeking out the best opportunities. Again, the liquidity the fund provides its investors will be a determining factor. The key is to avoid a mismatch between the terms offered to fund investors and the liquidity of the individual trades in the portfolio. The best PMs plan for the worst and assume liquid markets can turn illiquid in a flash, and set their position sizes accordingly.

FUNDS ARE BUSINESSES

Portfolio management responsibilities don't end with maintaining a vigilant eye on every trade in the portfolio.

PMs play an integral role in running the overall business, further stretching their time requirements and necessary skill set.

In addition to the investment decisions, PMs get involved in issues related to marketing, human resources, investor relations, compliance, legal, technology, risk management, and operations. There is usually a dedicated team of individuals to focus on each of these aspects of the business, but the PM is needed to support their efforts.

The marketing team, for example, will attempt to raise the profile of the firm by differentiating it from the rest of the competition. The PM is essential to the development of the "brand" and is often the person who speaks at industry conferences, promotes the organization in the media, and meets with current and potential investors. The PM works with the marketing team to formulate a way to articulate the core strategy of the fund and the investing principles that guide it.

The PM's investment guidelines are critical to the branding and answer the question of how the business expects to generate returns. They detail the markets where the firm will operate, the products it will trade, and what sort of volatility investors can expect. Is the goal to generate the highest possible annual returns, with less emphasis on potential losses, or is the aim to produce a consistent, modest return with low volatility? These factors distinguish one fund from another.

The hiring of traders and analysts, the creation of new funds, determining the terms in the fund offering memorandum, and choosing the execution venues are other responsibilities handled by the PM. In some situations, the PM is instrumental in determining the compensation for the various members of the investment team. Larger companies may have a CEO or a COO to help manage the day-to-day operations of the business, freeing up the PM to spend most of his or her time in the investing role. Even in this scenario, most major decisions will include some input from the PM.

Dealing with bruised egos is another responsibility. Traders and analysts can get anxious, and even angry, if they believe a PM is not utilizing any of their suggestions. After all, traders are evaluated on the effectiveness and profitability of their ideas. Compensation is largely contingent on their monetary contribution to the bottom line. A PM needs sound management skills to keep the team motivated and aligned with the best interests of the organization. Also, the PM needs to be a coach, providing constructive criticism when warranted and praise to others who are meeting expectations. These types of management issues once again highlight the importance of a well-developed EQ for a portfolio manager.

FOCUS ON THE INVESTMENT PROCESS

When I first started in the hedge fund business in the mid-1990s, the formula to get more assets under management was simple: generate good returns and investors—wealthy individuals and families—will find you. That formula worked when hedge funds were a novel concept and there wasn't a great deal of competition in the industry.

Today, there are more than 10,000 independent hedge funds with a combined total of $3 trillion in assets under management. According to Preqin, a global hedge fund research firm, there are now more than 5,000 institutions—including pension funds, endowments, and sovereign wealth funds—that invest in hedge funds. This institutionalization has brought a degree of standardization.[2]

As we discussed earlier in the book, institutional investors looking to allocate to hedge funds go through a due diligence process, which is a thorough examination of any firm they're considering. Due diligence is usually split into two components: operational and investment.

---

2   "2016 Preqin Global Hedge Fund Report—Sample Pages," 7, https://www.preqin.com/docs/samples/2016-Preqin-Global-Hedge-Fund-Report-Sample-Pages.pdf.

During operational due diligence, potential investors evaluate all matters related to the running of the business. They examine the disaster recovery and business continuity plan, learn the process by which the fund marks its books, review the compliance manual to comprehend internal policies and procedures, scour the fund's legal documents for any inconsistencies, and perform detailed background checks of the PMs and principals. They'll assess the stability and reputation of service providers, such as fund administrators, custodians, prime brokers, law firms, and third-party marketers. Two guys and a Bloomberg in a garage in Cleveland may be able to raise money from friends and family, but they're certainly not going to get an institutional allocation.

Investment due diligence is different. Here, investors try to understand how the PMs allocate capital. While this will include an investigation of historical performance, investors are more interested in whether or not the performance is repeatable. Investors don't want to look at the PM's investments so much as they want to scrutinize his or her investment *process*.

They ask a series of questions: What is the strategy of the fund? What is the performance target or benchmark? How are trade ideas sourced? How can the firm's "edge" and your expertise be demonstrated? How are ideas evaluated and analyzed? How are positions sized in the portfolio? How is risk monitored? How is it decided when to take profits, add to a position, or cut a trade in the portfolio? Who's responsible for trade execution, and how is it handled? They may ask several members of the team these questions to gauge how well the process is disseminated.

Investors will expect answers they are comfortable with before they entrust a PM with their capital. They may not follow the math or economics behind every trade, but they'll want to know the decision-making process. This process enables investors to compare one manager to another and defines the brand of the fund. The best PMs have a unique investment process they follow religiously and can clearly articulate it to investors. It's a method they stick with through thick and thin. It's what they rely on to help them get through the inevitable periods of below average performance.

PROTECTING THE BRAND

We discussed how the portfolio manager is responsible for promoting the fund's brand. The PM is in charge of protecting it as well. This means caring for and defending the firm's reputation at all times. It's the responsibility of the PM to ensure all investments are consistent with the mandate detailed in the fund's offering memorandum, or OM.

There are situations in which a PM will see an opportunity or want to trade in a market where the fund has not previously operated. It's true that most OMs are constructed to give the fund lots of legal flexibility when it comes to its investment mandate. Regardless, there is an implied contract between the investors and the PM to stick to what is often a much narrower focus. The OM may state that the fund can trade commodity futures, for example, but if the PM has marketed the fund as a merger arbitrage vehicle, investors will probably grow concerned if they see a coffee futures position in the portfolio. They may even take the drastic step of redeeming their entire investment. Style drift can ruin a hedge fund's reputation and lead to legal problems and regulatory headache.

Investors are willing to excuse losses, but they'll turn unforgiving when a fund loses money on an action that falls outside the stated directive. Investors can be equally harsh even if the trade was profitable. Despite their reputation as opaque when it comes to disclosure of positions, most funds are quite transparent, and investors make the effort to read the fund's commentary where details on how the fund made or lost money are provided. A good manager will never operate in areas outside the implied trading parameters of the fund without the advance permission of the investors. If there's one thing investors hate more than losses, it's surprises.

"[I'M LOOKING FOR] A 5:1 [PAYOFF]. FIVE TO ONE MEANS I'M RISKING ONE DOLLAR TO MAKE FIVE. WHAT FIVE TO ONE DOES IS ALLOW YOU TO HAVE A HIT RATIO OF 20 PERCENT. I CAN ACTUALLY BE A COMPLETE IMBECILE. I CAN BE WRONG 80 PERCENT OF THE TIME, AND I'M STILL NOT GOING TO LOSE."

In baseball, a hitter who reaches a base 30 percent of the time is deemed a star, and Jones holds that the same is true for investors. Paul Tudor Jones knows he doesn't have to win on every trade as long as he retains a consistent risk-reward ratio. He's humble about his ability to predict markets and uses superior risk management techniques to outperform other traders.

To protect the brand, a PM must not only intimately know every security in the portfolio, but also ensure all traders on the desk grasp the importance of sticking with the mandate and appreciate the extreme consequences for drifting outside it.

PORTFOLIO MANAGER AS PHILOSOPHER

An investment philosophy for a portfolio manager is a lot like a coaching philosophy for the coach of a sports team. Is the coach offense or defense-minded? Does the coach prefer to use every player on the bench or stick to a smaller rotation? A coach's philosophy continually evolves based on prior experience and accumulated knowledge of the sport, with a constant assessment of what is working and what needs adjustment. To be authentic, the coach's style will reflect his personality, values, and history. Of course, it will only work and be accepted by the players if presented in a transparent, objective-driven, and predictable manner. Constantly shifting the game plan will only leave the players confused.

Similarly, there's no single, definitive investment philosophy for everyone. Each investor needs to establish his or her own guidelines to play the investment game consistently. Investing without a philosophy is like steering a boat without a rudder. Random decision-making isn't a recipe for repeat performances and will generally lead to chaos.

An investor's philosophy should answer a series of fundamental questions regarding his or her opinion on the behavior of markets. Are markets efficient or inefficient? The answer to this question will likely lead to a preference for either an active or passive approach to investing. What are the risks and rewards of portfolio diversification? What is the tradeoff between minimizing risk and maximizing gain? Forming a personalized philosophy based on formal market understanding, experience, and individual behavioral tendencies is critical. It's much easier to make sound decisions inside such a framework.

Formal understanding is acquired through extensive research on markets, economics, and history. This research develops your market IQ. Read, read, read. An investor can study the opinion of Vanguard's John Bogle on the virtues of passive, market-cap weighted, diversified, indexed strategies. Then, for an opposing perspective, the investor can evaluate Warren Buffett's view that "Diversification is protection against ignorance. It makes little sense if you know what you're doing," a comment expressing the opinion that active investment management is right for some, but not right for others.

On this issue, John Bogle and Warren Buffett stand on two opposite sides. One is not necessarily right and the other wrong. One attitude may speak to a PM's personality, capabilities, or thought process more than the other does. The more you study and research markets, the more conviction you'll form towards various views on how markets work.

Experience is another major driver in establishing an investment philosophy. It attaches an emotional element to investing that can't be replicated through knowledge. It's what is responsible for developing your market EQ. Any market participant or seasoned investor can attest to the emotional pain associated with losing money through a bad trade or mistake. The errors, more often than the successes, form the philosophy's backbone. Someone who fully invested in technology stocks at the end of the 1990s and subsequently saw their gains evaporate may have formed a permanent view on whether markets are rational or irrational, or whether diversification is a friend or foe. Conversely, an investor with a long-term horizon and a conservative allocation going into that same period may have a contrasting opinion. Early successes or failures play a significant role in the creation of an investment philosophy.

Finally, behavioral tendencies are critical. Do you allow past experiences to change your future behavior? What is your risk tolerance? Are you, by nature, someone who follows the herd? Do you have a more value-driven, contrarian approach to investing, or do you prefer to follow the price action and momentum when committing capital? Appreciating your personal inclinations will help generate an investment philosophy consistent with your personality.

Every person has a unique combination of investment knowledge, market experiences, and behavioral tendencies. As a result, investors have different approaches to managing money. Formalizing these beliefs into a coherent philosophy is a cornerstone in creating an investment strategy. From that point forward, prospective investments should be judged on their consistency with the philosophy.

MY OWN PHILOSOPHY

This isn't a book focused on dispensing specific investment or trading advice. Such advice is prone to change frequently. I do think it's fair, though, to share elements of my philosophy toward money management, which is more immutable in nature. This doesn't mean that it never changes. It has evolved over the years. Today, my philosophy has more of an emphasis on investing rather than trading, which reflects my evolution from a short-term market maker on a trading desk to managing a multi-billion-dollar investment portfolio. This philosophy was developed over decades and reflects my aggregate knowledge, experience, and beliefs. Again, every investor is different. I only put it forward as an example.

1. **Investments should be examined and evaluated through three metrics: fundamental value, current valuation, and market sentiment.** The best opportunities result when these metrics align, meaning the investment is blessed with positive fundamentals, a relatively cheap valuation, and irrational negative sentiment.

2. **Asset allocation is more important than security selection.** Research indicates over 90 percent of the variability in investor returns is driven by the allocation to various asset classes, not individual security selection.

3. **Tactical asset allocation, if applied using a consistent framework, can add value to a portfolio.** Markets aren't efficient. Fundamentals, valuation, sentiment and, hence, expected returns, are in constant flux.

4. **Invest in areas you truly understand and know your limitations.** Accumulated knowledge is built up over many years and provides an advantage in the proper diligence of opportunities.

5. **The best opportunities come at the worst of times.** Contrarian thinking isn't the same as contrarian action. "Being greedy when others are fearful" as Warren Buffett said, dramatically improves expected long-term future returns.

6. **Knowing when to avoid the market is more valuable than knowing when to invest.** Treat cash as an asset class and avoid losses due to ill-timed allocations.

Most of my biggest investing blunders were preceded by a break from one of these tenets. At some point in my twenty-year career, I've violated each one of the above principles. More than it has helped me generate gains in the market, the philosophy has become critical in preventing costly mistakes. The school of hard knocks and its expensive tuition have taught me to spend more energy worrying about the downside to my actions than the upside.

If I had to pick one axiom from the list that should appear in the personal philosophy of all investors, it would be the one pertaining to investing in markets and products that you truly understand. Whenever I have dabbled in trading or investing in a market beyond my existing skill set, the results were usually poor. Looking back, I'd attribute any small amount of success to luck. Experts aren't created overnight, and thinking you can out-trade or out-analyze experts when blindly going into unknown areas is a fool's game.

CONCLUSION

A healthy dose of humility towards the market is essential to successful trading. I'm not saying that every thriving trader is humble—far from it—but the best ones understand their importance relative to the market. Legendary investors can come across as brash, arrogant, and overconfident, but I can assure you that their approach when trading is quite different.

In 2009, I was fortunate enough to be selected to join an esteemed committee run by the Federal Reserve Bank of New York. I'd begun discussions with representatives from the Fed earlier that year in response to their desire to better comprehend what was happening in the market during the financial crisis. Back then, the Fed didn't have adequate resources to monitor markets effectively. They were behind the curve when it came to acknowledging the depth of the crisis. Rather than going to their usual intelligence source—the banks—they started to seek out individual investors who had detailed knowledge of different markets.

The person who covered us at Goldman Sachs connected me with somebody from the Fed who wanted to discuss the mortgage market. I spent hours on the phone with multiple Fed representatives discussing the impact of credit default swaps, collateralized debt obligations, and other esoteric products. Soon, the Fed realized the benefit of reaching out to a broader investment community. They formed a committee of such people called the Investor Advisory Committee on Financial Markets, or the IACFM. I was honored to be one of its founding members.

A group of approximately a dozen money managers from the hedge fund, pension fund, private equity, endowment, and traditional asset management community met each quarter at the Federal Reserve offices in New York, with an equal number of Fed representatives present. Timothy Geithner, the president of the New York Fed at the time, was the original chairman of the committee. After Geithner stepped down to head the Treasury Department, Bill Dudley took over the committee as the next president of the New York Fed.

In the meetings, we talked about the state of the financial markets and the global economy with the goal of alerting the Fed to any potential systemic risks we may have identified.

The committee was a who's who of the investment management business. Mohamed El-Erian (PIMCO), Louis Bacon (Moore), David Tepper (Appaloosa), Jim Chanos (Kynikos), Rick Rieder (BlackRock), and Josh Harris (Apollo) are just some of the luminaries who sat on this committee. I admit to having felt a little out of place, especially since I was the youngest person in the room by a wide margin.

I learned a great deal over the course of the five years I spent on the committee. Perhaps the most valuable insight I took away was an appreciation for the similarities and differences among these successful investors.

The members of the IACFM had certain traits in common. For example, everybody shared a relative humility about his or her ability to predict market behavior. It was rare for someone to present a point of view without numerous qualifications. That doesn't mean they lacked conviction. Rather, they appreciated the possibility of being wrong. In fact, they tended to spend more time discussing how they could be wrong than how they could be right.

Another similarity among the committee members was the broad range of topics in which they could converse. Each investor had intimate knowledge of their market of expertise, but they could easily participate in discussions about other markets, politics, regulatory issues, or the investment business as a whole. These people weren't just traders or portfolio managers; they were business leaders.

Not everybody shared the same views on world events, and heated discussions broke out at many of the meetings. Every investor on the committee had a unique skill set, philosophy, and investment process that contributed to his or her success.

Mohamed El-Erian, as previously discussed, is somebody who can synthesize complicated macro issues into a coherent narrative. Many of his forecasts and conclusions were medium- and longer-term in nature. He avoided short-term predictions. His strength, developed from his years at the IMF and as the head of the Harvard endowment, produced insightful long-term perspectives on issues. To guide him through the markets, he relied on his superior knowledge of monetary and government policy, as well as his formal economics training.

David Tepper operates in an entirely different manner. While he is surely capable of understanding long-term consequences of the various policy decisions, he focuses less on the theoretical and more on the practical components of markets. When making predictions, he evaluates sentiment, flows, and positioning. He also holds an extremely high degree of common sense. He doesn't make his market analysis more complicated than necessary. He filters through the noise better than anybody I've met. He is blessed with the ability to trade with conviction. To use a line from the Kenny Rogers hit "The Gambler," Tepper knows when to hold 'em, when to fold 'em, when to walk away, and when to run. This special skill has made him arguably the best discretionary hedge fund manager ever.

Louis Bacon is also unique in that his approach to trading is more old school. He didn't appear interested in predicting monetary policy, or the long-term viability of the Eurozone. He gets most of his information from prices, not opinions. He's humble enough to appreciate that markets move for a variety of reasons. Rather than justifying behavior with cute narratives, he obtains his information from observing trends and flows. Quantitative data is more highly valued than qualitative inputs. His unique skill is being able to "read the tape" and respect prices. This emphasis on price action contributes to his effectiveness as a risk manager. It's a lot easier to cut a position when you aren't hanging on to some fundamental belief of what *should* happen as opposed to what *is* happening.

Each of these investors, along with other members of the committee, has a unique approach to trading and investing. What makes them successful is the ability to identify their edge, whether its capacity to synthesize complicated macroeconomic issues into actionable investment themes, the capability to withstand the pressure of moving against the consensus, or having outstanding discipline when it comes to risk management. Their advantages weren't developed overnight. They came as the result of countless hours of study and practice.

Still, nobody bats a thousand, as I witnessed firsthand.

In 2012, in the midst of the European crisis, the Fed advisory committee met for its quarterly meeting. The widespread view at the time was that Greece and Spain would default on their debt, forcing them out of the European Union and leading to a banking crisis similar to that of 2008.

The Fed, which was concerned about the spillover effects of a European default, wanted the group's opinion on the potential ramifications such a default could have on the global economy. They were particularly worried about the impact it may have on US markets and financial conditions. Elevated volatility showed the risk of a systemic event was real. The heavyweights of the industry sitting in the meeting all held negative outlooks, and discounted the ability of the European authorities to resolve the situation. Virtually the entire group was in agreement—for once—when asked by the Fed how the bubbling crisis affected their own market positioning. Nobody wanted to take risk. The consensus view was that the situation was going to get worse before it got better. Most proclaimed to be short or sitting on the sidelines.

A few days after the meeting, out of the blue, everyone was proven wrong. Mario Draghi, the president of the European Central Bank (ECB), was delivering a speech in London at the Global Investment Conference. Halfway through his speech, he uttered a phrase that shocked the markets: "Within our mandate, the ECB is ready to do whatever it takes to preserve the euro. And believe me, it will be enough." This sentence changed the course of the Eurozone.

The ECB ended up adopting quantitative easing (QE) measures many thought were impossible. The QE announcement, and Germany agreeing to the measures, caught the markets by surprise. It marked the end of the crisis, and the beginning of a European recovery.

Right before the declaration of quantitative easing, most investors had exited the markets and taken their losses.

The uncertainty was just too high to hold on at that point. With all the forced sellers out of the way, prices weren't going to drop any lower. When the information flow turned positive, investors were compelled to come back in and repurchase what they'd recently sold. It was like the OJ futures pit in *Trading Places*.

All of us investors on the committee, including the Fed, had access to the best data, intelligence, consultants, and contacts at other central banks, yet we still got it wrong. Markets really do move in the direction to screw the most people.

What is the moral of the above story? Even if you have the credentials to be selected as an advisor to the New York Fed, you're not always going to be right. We're all subjected to behavioral biases, poor or inadequate analysis, and all the other causes of bad decision-making and misguided investments. Again, the need for humility can't be over-emphasized. It's difficult to thrive in this business, even for the most accomplished hedge fund managers. The capacity for good judgment is not formed overnight.

Passion for the industry and personal development are the only ways to overcome these challenges. For everyone in the hedge fund trading world, whether it's the person trying to break in, or the twenty-year vet who is an industry influencer, the career is about hard work, discipline, commitment, and a little bit of luck. Passion for pushing through the rejection and the obstacles is what keeps people in the game and helps them avoid the notorious attrition. There are always ways to advance your knowledge and improve your mental performance. But it takes effort.

The actor Will Smith describes his ability to advance in Hollywood—an equally competitive industry—in the following way:

"You're not going to out-work me. It's such a simple, basic concept. The guy who is willing to hustle the most is going to be the guy that just gets that loose ball. The majority of people who aren't getting the places they want or aren't achieving the things that they want in this business is strictly based on hustle. It's strictly based on being out-worked; it's strictly based on missing crucial opportunities. I say all the time if you stay ready, you ain't gotta get ready."[1]

In other words, you have to wake up every morning ready to bite the ass off a bear.

---

1   "Will Smith> Quotes> Quotable Quotes," http://www.goodreads.com/
     quotes/281801-the-only-thing-that-i-see-that-is-distinctly-different.

The reason I wrote this book was to give pertinent advice to those looking to get into the industry. Additionally, I wanted to dispel some of the negative stereotypes associated with a trading career by providing a behind-the-scenes look at the realities of the business. I've seen too many young, talented individuals begin a trading career, only to discover later they lacked the appropriate personality or underestimated the effort required to thrive. Finally, I wanted to give encouragement to those who lack the typical pedigree to get through the front door of a hedge fund. My background and experience prove no school or network has a monopoly on candidates with passion and desire.

If your dream is to be a trader, and you've done an honest self-assessment whose results support the dream, then stick with it. Don't let anybody tell you it's not possible. Your dream is one position you should never cut.

ABOUT THE AUTHOR

PHOTO: JOSH RITCHIE

GARTH FRIESEN started his finance career in 1994 when, after completing his MBA from the Ivy School of Business at the University of Western Ontario, he went to work for Merrill Lynch in London, United Kingdom, as an interest rate swaps trader. After two years of working as a market-maker at Merrill, he moved to UBS with several colleagues to join their proprietary trading group. At UBS, Garth developed his skill in the niche area of relative value trading.

He was introduced to III Capital Management in 1998, the well-known hedge fund management company founded in 1982 that specializes in relative value trading in the fixed income and volatility markets. Over the years, he has traded numerous interest rate products in different markets around the globe. Garth has specific experience trading Danish mortgage bonds, U.S. Treasuries, agency mortgages, municipal derivatives, basis swaps, and interest rate swaps and options.

In 2005, he helped III Capital enter the credit business, launching a relative value credit fund for the firm. He was the portfolio manager and oversaw trading of investment grade and high yield corporate bonds, structured credit, non-agency mortgages and all credit derivatives. Following the successful launch of a long/short credit vehicle and a short credit fund in 2007, he became the co-CIO along with the company's founder, Cliff Viner. During his tenure as co-CIO, he served as a member for five years on the esteemed New York Fed's Investor Advisory Committee on Financial Markets, advising senior management on financial, economic, and public policy issues. He has also been featured in various media, including CNBC, Bloomberg, and *The Wall Street Journal*, among others.

Garth lives in Boca Raton, Florida, the headquarters for III Capital Management. He is married to his wife, Jeannie, and is a father to three teenage children, two girls and a boy. In his spare time, he is an active member of a local Rotary Club and still maintains his Canadian roots by playing hockey every week.

Made in the USA
San Bernardino, CA
20 June 2017